I0624110

Contents

Shoe Facts 1

Shoe Colors 18

My Shoe Attraction 34

A Shoe Sale 43

A Shoe Closet 57

Shoe Magic 66

Shoe Secrets 80

A Walk in My Shoes 94

A Shoe Book 103

THE MAGIC OF SHOES

A Journey Through Middle School With The Right Pair Of Shoes.

For people who walk through life looking for a direction; either up or down, this way and that, straight or crooked, but whichever way shoes are a part of our daily lives. A pair of shoes can be a hint to how much one earns, what kind of job one obtains, or a glimpse of one's personality. Some people, adults and, children, may never get the chance to experience the magical feeling of wearing a new pair of shoes. Some kids may never understand the importance that shoes have made in history. By telling the story, The Magic of Shoes will help middle school students understand the trials and tribulations of life as a young adult. Teenagers are given one chance to develop a sense of pride and self-confidence that will hopefully shape their outlook on growing up. The Magic of Shoes shares stories with twists and turns, about what happens in middle school, answers questions about making choices, and promotes analytical thinking skills.

When Sheba puts on shoes a magical spirit appears around her. Sheba was born in North America, but her father and ancestors live in West Africa. Sheba's family celebrated her birth with a new pair of baby shoes and every birthday after that. When she puts on new shoes for the first time, they create a magical spirit that stays with her for life. Sheba gets excited about new shoes, but on her sixth birthday, something happened. She visited family in Ghana, West Africa, and was welcomed with a pair of sandals. Sheba was happy as she opened her gift not knowing what was inside. When she opened the gift, bright sparks flared into the air, and she thought about what type of magic sandals are they and what will they do. When Sheba put on her feet into those sandals something happened, and she started crying. The sandals were different from American sandals; they looked different, felt different, and smelled different. New shoes give Sheba personality that creates a persona to make good choices for understanding her life. The style and color of each pair of shoes gives her expression, attitude, and self-determination. Each chapter explores a view of Sheba developing a positive relationship through decisions she makes through the love of magic shoes.

Shoe Facts

My mother always tells elaborate tales before she tucks my sister and me in bed at night, stories that make us think about the importance of our heritage and culture. She always starts her stories with facts about the origin of shoes, and always ends with, "It is a privilege to have shoes!" During early civilization, if your private parts were covered you were happy, and covering the feet was not a concern. Through my mother's stories, I've learned that many cultures endure extreme weather (in frigid temperatures or the sweltering heat) without the proper footwear, and yet no one complains. How were they able to deal with that, I wondered? Mom said, "They didn't know what shoes were back then". Why, I asked curiously, mother and *La-La* looks at me and reply in unison, "It was the beginning of time don't you get it". I just shook my head and asked mom to tell me more and she continued, "About two million years ago during the Stone Age, the Paleolithic times", mom looks at me and says, "That is prehistory before humans evolved, and when the Hominine ancestors of human beings, including Australopithecus, Homo Habilis, Homo Erectus and Homo Ergaster roamed the earth". Mom breaks out with a high-pitched laugh as she tries to pronounce all the prehistoric words. She continued, "They roamed most of the earth and began making the first stone tools that led to a bright idea of footwear. Sandals were most common and the first footwear to be developed".

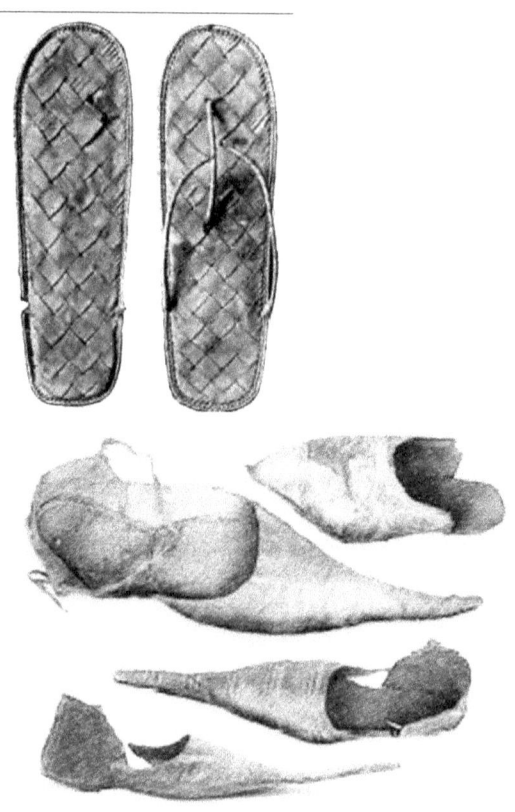

My mother always impressed me with her shoe stories and knowledge, sometimes she tells the same story when buying new shoes. That's to make sure my sister and I understand that it's a privilege to have new shoes. Other stories mom told were, shoes are more than something you wear on your feet they tell something about who you are. Because the story of shoes was told over and over since my very first pair, I consider shoes a wonderful and fashionable accessory that is necessary in order to walk through life. I think about... what if shoes were only for the rich people, the privileged ones, then I would be just like my father walking barefoot. I can't imagine walking barefooted through a muddy path, a rocky stream, or a wet ground like my father did in Africa. He never questioned not having shoes because everyone in his village didn't either; it was normal. When his family goes to the market, when he was outside playing, or going to school dad walks without shoes on. My dad said his feet would often bleed, a cut here and there, so he used any available water to clean his feet. It was customary not to complain, and with one foot in front of the other, he continued his journey of walking.

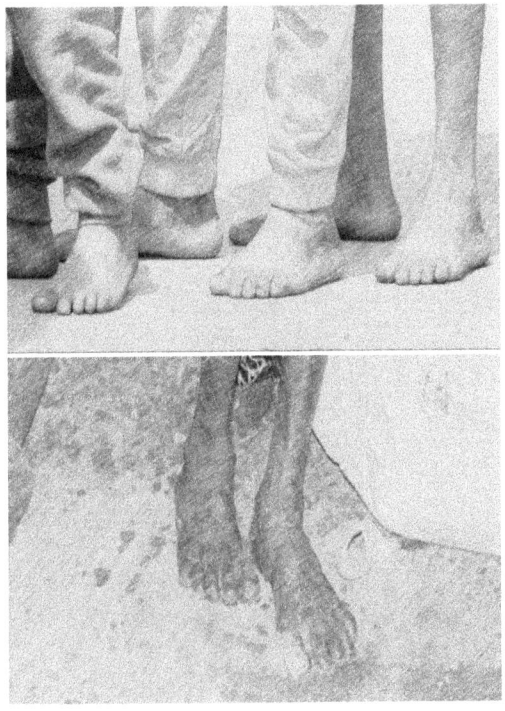

Shoes have been around for a very long time from what I now know as a middle school student, and without a variety of shoes, footwear was very simple, and less complicated than shoes are today in 2016. The last thing people worried about back then was their feet, but today people must have a shoe collection. Shoe categories that classify shoe types go beyond footwear that was designed just to protect the feet. It's an item of decoration that is worn for style to give fashion a statement. The design elements of fashion in cultures around the world have created various shoe options in high and flat heels, which are now made with expensive materials and complex construction. Shoes can sell for as little as one dollar or as much as a few thousand of dollars a pair, and selling shoes can be a successful career option. I enjoy shoe facts as I compare them to my world history class because there is always a beginning with no end in sight. Although Italy is the shoe capital of the world, China is the world's biggest shoe manufacturer with many factories for making shoes, apparel, and other items. Products, including shoes, are made for companies like; Nike, Coach, and Nine West to name a few. They also specialize in producing high quality materials for leather boots and industrial shoes that are reasonably priced. The problem is the duplication of the original products are relabeled and sold as knockoffs, which are unauthorized by the company to produce and sell. Either shoes, sneakers, bags, belts, or clothing are made from fewer quality materials then the original. It's the same concept as cloning, and a very big business called counterfeiting, which is now illegal in America but it still happens through the black market, and sold around the world. There are shoe manufacturing plants in America, so I asked mom if we can make plans to visit one day. I want to see how shoes are made, which will be so exciting for me and La-La. After visiting so many shoe stores it will be cool to see the process from start to finish, then I could share my shoe stories with others.

The human foot remains unchanged after thousands of years, believe it or not! What people wear on their feet shows universal diversity without knowing how a culture thrives. Through this diversity is how tradition is made within a family, and the most interesting aspects of culture is revealed. There are wonderful shoe museums that share stories of culture by displaying exhibitions of shoes. I enjoy the virtual versions of a shoe exhibition as it gives the history of shoes on display. As you enter these exhibitions, prepare to step into someone else's shoes, and see the world from a different perspective. Looking at footwear through a historical timeline display shoes on a journey from 4,500 years of footwear fantasy; is a visual evolution right before your eyes. This timeline shows methods, materials, and tools that were used to create all type of shoes. This exhibit starts with of course sandals, Chinese silk shoes, and couture pumps, and with one-of-a-kind designs. Shoes emerged as essential fashion accessories that are no longer hidden by the garment. Over a century ago, visionaries' influences on fashion change every decade in response to design, politics, and social change. When I think about footwear and its purpose I see shoes as being both ordinary and extraordinary with one main purpose, to protect the foot from injury. Footwear is now developed into many forms with unique ways to satisfy the need for appropriate footwear, and a requirement for employment. Shoes are considered beauty as they create identity, pride, and diversity. Some of the first shoes were moccasins made with natural dyes, pigments, smoked moose hide, caribou skin, and colorful symmetrical embroidery or not. The Native Americans in the 1800s used many different resources and methods was used to create footwear such as black buckskin, and beads. It also involved oxidizing pulp of the walnut to create color, and all-natural resources (of course) was used as they were abundant.

I've never thought of shoes as being a part of art, and shoemakers have inspired artists to be creative. Mom started teaching us about shoes, and now I have a few things to teach her as I am learning more and more about footwear. Like, elegant shoes are the high heels with many shapes of this style is considered a work of art. When I look at shoes as art I try to make sense of them; like a golden drinking cup in the shape of a boot, shoes and tools used to construct a shoemaker's outfit, or shoelaces used for a belt, and a shoe hat is quite ridiculous I thought, but that's art they say. How about boots that are so tight it took a day to put them on as they will never come off without help. What about wearing steel-toed work boots made out of clay, but they look like the real thing one would say. Shoes displaying a different era are nice to see like; the roaring twenties, a T-bar shoe with buckles, bows, and straps. These type of shoes is available through a special order, but very expensive. The twenties era is when shoes really made a name for themselves, which gave them a future. In the thirties, shoes began to look heavier, less pointed, and more rounded but not squared. Wedge heel designs were created in Italy, and then came a wedge platform shoe with a thicker sole started to emerge into society. In the sixties and seventies was the retro era, and that style was platforms shoes, bell bottoms, and everything was funky. Shoes are made for all occasions and for all groups and cultures of people; they provide a uniform look, and sometimes comfort.

My great grandma told me before she passed away about the big band era, which was shoe fashion popularity in American between 1935 and 1945. Having the right shoes was important as wearing the right dress or suit. All people cared about was having an awareness of how shoes looked on their feet, and coordinating their outfit with them. The big change in shoe fashion was having more shoe options, and sizes available like never before from designers around the world. A custom fit shoe changed the way Americans viewed fashion by having a pair of shoes for all occasions. New and popular shoes were high-heel sandals, lace-up shoes, and wedges that are making a comeback after they were first introduced. For men; loafers, slip on sandals, conservative or lace-up shoes, and of course sneakers are always popular. Leather continues to be used for boots and shoes with buckets and fringes seen on them. The color choices during this era were neutral colors like tan, brown and black. Then multicolor shoes were also introduced with lace, embroidery, beads, and rhinestone. I am glad I didn't have to live through that era, it seems so boring; everyone getting excited over nothing.

Then in 1984 Chucks and AF1's (Airforce one) started the era of basketball shoes. The invention of basketball shoes called sneakers was not by accident. Sneakers were invented to meet a need, but in 1984 Michael Jordan created the Jordan era, and sneakers were never the same again. Jordan sneakers took over the basketball court, and every kid in school wanted a pair. Jordan's ruled the air in the golden era (1994 to 1998) with new technologies, materials, and design concepts for basketball shoes were produced thanks to MJ. Then the throwback era started in 1991with Jordan's second retirement. All the boys at school have Jordan brand sneakers, and think they are super cool because those sneakers are expensive. If I had a brother mom won't even think about buying him a pair, then he would have issues of not being popular. I'm working on setting up an interactive board that will display facts about shoes because kids and adults know nothing about the history of shoes. Most people only have a basic knowledge of buying shoes, and find it difficult when choosing a color, size, style, or brand. Shoe history, facts, and tips should be displayed in stores where consumers can learn what's trending in the shoe world. I think online shopping gives more variety and availability of styles, colors, and size making the shopping experience fun. Shoes are made from rubber, plastics, and other petrochemical derived materials (petrochemicals are chemical products from petroleum). Some chemical compounds made from petroleum are also obtained from other fossil fuels, such as coal, natural gas, or renewable sources like corn and sugar cane, so it's safe to wear. The foot contains more bones than any part of the body, which can be easily broken without proper balance.

The shoe facts and tips display board will exhibit all sorts of valuable information and visuals that brings attention to the history of footwear, which is the perfect display for any museum or gallery. The boards will be all dressed up in bright colors, and with my cousin Marie's artistic touch I'm sure people will be talking it up. I'm hoping to go viral once I create a social media link.

Footwear Facts

Sandals originated due to warm climates, so the feet need protection from the hot ground, Although the top of the feet was exposed they are safe from injury.

4,000 years ago the first shoes were made out of a single piece of rawhide that enveloped the foot for both warmth and protection.

In Europe, pointed toes on shoes were fashionable from the eleventh to the fifteenth century.

In the Middle East heels were added to
lift the foot from the burning sand.

In Europe during the sixteenth and seventeenth
Century when heels were added to shoes they

were always colored red.
Shoes all over the world were identical until the

nineteenth century when left- and right-footed
shoes were first made in Philadelphia.

In Europe it wasn't until the eighteenth century

that women's shoeswere different from men's.

Six-Inch-high heels were worn by the upper classes
in seventeenth-century Europe. Two servants, one on
either side, was needed to hold up the person
wearing the high heels.

Sneakers were made in America in 1916,
and they were originally called Keds.

Boots were first worn in cold mountainous regions,

and hot sandy deserts where horse-riding communities lived. Heels on boots kept feet secure in the stirrups.

The first lady's boot was designed for Queen Victoria in 1840.

SHOES AS SYMBOLS

- Biblical times a sandal was given as a sign of an oath.

- At the wedding, the groom handed the bride a shoe, which she put on to show she was then his subject.

- In China one of the bride's red shoes is tossed from the roof to ensure happiness for the couple.

- In Hungary the groom drinks a toast to his bride out of her wedding slipper.

- Mmm..In America when a couple is married a pair of shoes is tied to the bumper of the couple's car.

- 2uIn the Middle Ages a father passed his authority over his daughter, and to her husband in a shoe ceremony.

I would love to host a shoe exhibit for children at the Art Gallery and provide hands on crafts and activities. This experience will give children a sense of why shoes are important as they are building social skills. There will be a question and answer session to allow critical thinking that gets kids talking about their feelings, and discuss wearing shoes for different reasons. Some of the questions I will ask for discussion are…

1. Do you remember wearing your first pair of shoes?
2. How does new shoes make you feel?
3. Would you like to choose your own pair of shoes?
4. What are your favorite colors of shoes?
5. Why do we wear shoes?
6. What would you do if you had no shoes?

Hands on activities give children social interaction that they enjoy, so I will provide shoe string, glitter, and stencils with large shoe cut outs in different categories of footwear. There will be sandals, slippers, dress-up shoes, high and low heel shoes, sports shoes, golf shoes, baseball shoes, running shoes, fashion boots, boots for riding and construction, painter shoes, snow shoes, work shoes, nursing shoes, shoes for dancing, ballet or tap, flippers for scuba diving or snorkeling, and specialty shoes. There will be children shoes on display for touching and trying on. I will enhance their sensory by having them to polish shoes, and keep them engaged in the activity. I will have several IPad's available to let children play online games, and move them to one activity to another. One online game I like is called fancy shoes; little kids can decorate a new pair of shoes for Franny who's going to a party. http://www. sproutonline.com/games/fancy-shoes. The first choice for this game is selecting a color for Franny's shoes then the decorations, which there are lots to choose from. At the end of the game Franny's shoes come alive then she puts on her brand new shoes and goes to the dance party. I will read the story; there was an old woman who lived in a shoe, she had so many shoes she didn't know what to do. Each participant will take home a shoe bag with printable coloring pages, reward charts, certificates, a shoe story and a measurement chart, game apps, and do at home crafts. I interviewed my dance instructor to learn more about shoe facts as he started off with a timeline.

A Timeline of Shoes

4000 BC – First archeological evidence of protective foot covering found in Ice Age settlements.

4000 BC – First recorded mentioning of shoes as "flexible pieces of leather" came from Ancient Egypt.

3627 BC – Archeologist found the earliest known leather shoe near one of the cave dwellings in Armenia.

3rd to 1st Millennia BC – Many civilizations around the world used simple leather sandals in their daily life.

Egyptian Pharaoh Tutankhamen carried to his tomb exquisite sandals that were engraved with beautiful golden pictures of gods and religious symbols.

1st Millennia BC – Romans used platform sandals made from wood or cork soles. Buskin shoes were also common in Greece and Rome, where they were worn by tragic actors, hunters and soldiers.

Around 1000 AD – Shoes and sandals become common place across Europe, but they are often crude and hard to wear for long periods of time. Saxon wedding ritual which the bride throws one of her shoe behind her back to determine which of her bridesmaids will be married next was born.

12th and 13th Century – Fashionable shoes started being produced for nobility and royalty. Their designs started focusing on extending the toes section, the larger the toes the more they represented wearers rank.

16th Century – Renaissance and the rise of wealthy class people marked the beginning of the widespread of footwear fashion.

1533 – Italian noblewoman Catherine D'Medici introduced to France fashion of high heels.

1789 – French Revolution brought to the end the fashion of high heeled man and female footwear, and popularized more "down to earth" designs.

1790 – English inventors introduced shoelaces for the first time.

1800 – In the 19th Century shoes were made for each foot individually. Before that the majority of footwear could be used with both feet's (called "straight" shoes).

1883 – African American inventor Jan Ernst Matzeliger invented a machine for the automated production of shoes. This invention changed the shoe industry forever.

1888 – First high heeled shoe factory opened in United States.

This event enabled American females to largely abandon imported expensive shoes from France.

1899 – Irish-American inventor Humphrey O'Sullivan successfully patented rubber heel for shoes.

1917 – The first successful sneakers (canvas top design with rubber sole) started being sold in United States. They received the name because of their lightness and silence that was provided by soft rubber. They were initially used by kids and tennis players.

1955 – High "comma" heels or "Stiletto" heels was invented in Italy by the French fashion designer Roger Vivier.

Stiletto became extremely popular across the female population of the world.

1950s and Beyond – Introduction of advanced rubber, plastic, synthetic cloth, and industrial materials enabled the creation of many new shoe designs.

1980 – Athletic shoes that were first introduced in early 20th Century became widely popular across the world.

Amazing information and something I never knew about in the history of shoes. When people buy shoes it would be great if the sales person has knowledge of shoe history. Split sole shoes are designed with a sole in two sections, rather than a solid piece that covers the bottom of the feet like most shoes. Split soles include a heel pad and a toe pad, often made from a rough material to provide traction. The center of the shoe is left without a sole, and with only the soft material at the bottom for protecting the feet. Split soles are not made for long-term purposes, so I will consider them specialty shoes. This style of shoe has advantages and disadvantages as all shoes do, and just like everything else in life there is good and bad shoes too. One of the biggest advantages of split sole shoes are; they create more flexibility in the foot making it easier for traction on difficult surfaces. Split toe shoes allows the feet to feel the ground as they provide less arch support. They are not always ideal for prolonged outdoor wear, as the soft section in the middle of the shoe is vulnerable to rocks, and other hard objects that can hurt the foot. Split sole shoes are seen as an option for dancing such as ballet and jazz. Some people who work outdoors also wear split sole shoes, like climbers and hunters, because they want to feel more of a connection with the terrain. Navigating for traction allows a person to curve his or her foot for a greater grip. Split toe shoes are quieter, which is great for hunters as they do not want to alert their prey. It's important to get a proper fit on the foot because this type of shoe should not be too loose as the result may not be as flexible, and the fit should not be extremely tight or it will be very uncomfortable. I have two pairs of the same style shoes, one in black the other in brown. I love these shoes so much I wear them even though they are too small because they are a perfect match for my skirts. Sometimes when I buy shoes without trying them on I order by my size, but when they arrive at my doorstep and I invite them in the shoes don't fit. After wearing the shoes for hours trying to make them fit, my feet pains me then I take them off to walk barefoot. Buying shoes online is risky business unless you want to waste time sending them back. When trying on shoes in the store, it's a good idea to walk around first then curve and point them to see how the shoe responds to your feet before buying them making sure you feel no pain.

It's no secret that everyone has foot problems at some point in life, but don't see a foot doctor when there's pain. I went to visit a foot doctor, or a Podiatrist as they are called, to learn about the anatomy of the foot; the best way to learn something is hands on. I thought it would be fun to learn some foot care facts to share with others, and to increase my shoe knowledge. I was handed a 3-D picture of the foot, and I learned…

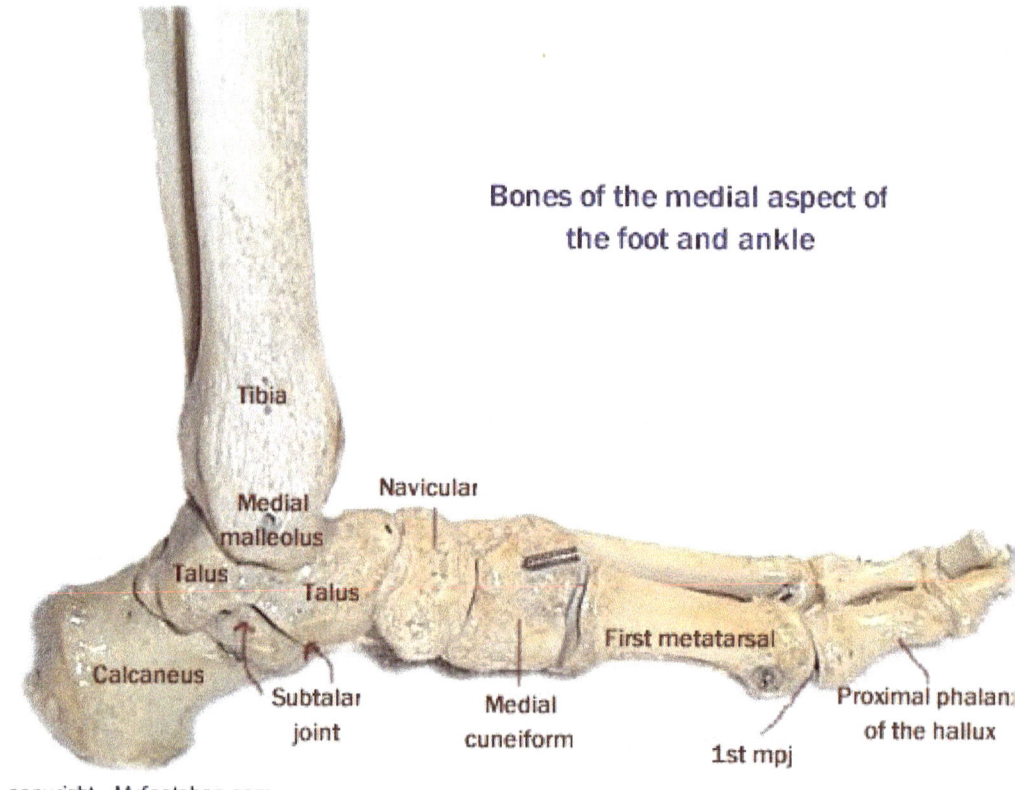

Bones of the medial aspect of the foot and ankle

Tibia

Navicular

Medial malleolus

Talus

Talus

First metatarsal

Calcaneus

Subtalar joint

Medial cuneiform

1st mpj

Proximal phalanx of the hallux

copyright - Myfootshop.com

- The human foot and ankle is a strong mechanical structure that contains 26 bones, 33 joints, more than 107 ligaments and 19 muscles tendons.

- There are 52 bones in your feet that make up one quarter of all the bones in your body. When they are out of alignment, so is the rest of your body.

- There are 250,000 sweat glands in both feet, and they excrete up to half a pint of moisture each day.

- The soles of your feet contain more sweat glands and sensory nerve endings per square centimeter than any other part of the body.

- Buying shoes is best done during the afternoon because the feet tend to swell a little during the day, so it's best to buy shoes that fit then.

- Women are four times more likely to have foot problems than men, mostly due to high heel shoes.

- A 2½-inch high heel can increase the load on the forefoot by 75%.

- Many people have one foot that is larger than the other, so it's best to fit the larger foot while standing.

- The average person takes 8,000 to 10,000 steps a day, which adds up to 115,000 miles in a lifetime – more than four times the circumference of the globe.

- An average day of walking, the total forces on your feet can total hundreds of tons, is equivalent to a fully loaded cement truck.

- Walking is the best exercise for your feet. It contributes to your general health by improving circulation and weight control.

- Standing in one spot is far more tiring than walking because the demands are being made on the same few muscles for a longer length of time.

- Foot ailments can become your first sign of more serious medical problems. Your feet mirror your general health, so conditions like arthritis, diabetes, nerve and circulatory disorders can show their initial symptoms in your feet.

- Arthritis is the number one cause of disability in America, including in your feet.

- Podiatric Physicians are four times less likely to use costly services than other physicians.

Do you know…

- 75% of Americans will experience foot problems at one time or another.

- 19% of the US population has an average of 1.4 foot problems each year.

- 5% of the US population has fungal foot infections each year.

- 5% of the US population has in grown toe nail problems each year.

- 5% of the US population has corns or calluses each year, and people are less likely to receive treatment and more likely to continue having problems without treatment.

- 6% of US population has foot injuries, bunions, flat feet or fallen arches each year.

- 60% of all foot & ankle injuries aged 17 or older are ankle strains or sprains.

- 60-70% of diabetics will develop some form of diabetic nerve damage, which in severe forms can lead to diabetic lower limb amputation.

Approximately 56,000 people a year lose their foot or leg due to diabetes. Heel pain and in grown toe nails are the most common problems. Tarsal Tunnel Syndrome is a very common and the reason for feeling pain as well as burning in the feet, and only a small percentage of the population is born with foot problems. It is neglect and a lack of awareness of proper care including ill-fitting shoes that bring on foot problems. Walking barefoot can cause plantar warts, and a virus can enter through a cut.

Shoe Colors

The tradition of shoes has come a long way and I can't imagine having only one style (the sandal), one pair, or one color. With every new pair of shoes I was given either as a gift, or just because it was time for new pair I always wanted colorful shoes. I remember growing up and really getting excited about going to the shoe store. *La-La* was ok with the basic colors of black, brown, and every once and while she would get blue. I cried when I was two years old because I wanted to pick out my own style and color of shoes, but mom wanted to make all the choices for me. Mom couldn't understand why I screamed as if a needle stuck me when the shoe clerk was fitting me in black shoes. I would try on all the black and blue shoes in the store, and nothing satisfied me then mom told the clerk to try me on the sparkly red pair and the sunshine yellow pair. I thought I was Dorothy trying to follow the yellow brick road as I imagined wearing ruby red shoes. Then mom said, "Take them off her!" and she asked for white or tan shoes only. At two, three, four, and five years old mom won, but she didn't know how much her decisions for my footwear would change my life. Mom still doesn't know how I feel at fifteen about not allowing me to make shoe choices when I was young. It affected my attitude and self-esteem, and as a result I have a secret relationship with shoes that no one knows about.

Shoe color is an important factor in my life as it creates my attitude, choices, and the ability to express myself through a color vision. I guess that's why I was not allowed to make my own color choices to express my personality. That's right, kids have personality they are empowered to think in this digital age of electronics and social media through iPads, iPhones, and gaming systems. Color is the visual perceptual property corresponding in humans through categories called red, blue, yellow, green, etc. The process of mixing colors are simply done to create new colors. I learned all about mixing colors in first grade, believe it or not. When mixing equal parts of two different colors it produce a certain shade from the prime color, then it gets real technical after that. Color vision and concepts are needed for comparison and measurement, which is all about a person's color vision that coordinates with many parts of the human eye. I tried to explain this to my mother and sister when I was six years old. Of course they thought I was a little strange for knowing that information. When I see a rainbow, and I love rainbows, I always say God is smiling at the world and he's happy, I haven't seen one lately. A rainbow is a separation of colors by a prism that consist of primary and secondary colors, and a continuous range of spectral colors. Wow… a rainbow is caused by refraction and a reflection in falling water droplets. I now understand why I see color through visible light. I think I have a high color vision IQ. The timeline of color is long, but what I learned is that I love all shades of it.

It is important to know what shoes to wear with jeans, dresses, skirts, suits, shorts, slacks, uniforms, and swimwear. Shoes must be matched to wedding attire, gym clothes, play sets, club,formal, work, and casual attire. Because there are so many shoe color combinations to select from it excites me in so many ways. Explaining this to mom is way beyond her color vision, and she doesn't understand why I am driven by a higher force to be a color coordinator. At least I can talk to *La-La* she listens to me. I already know her color vision, which is very limited. Everyone always ask, what's my favorite color, but I don't have one so I say all colors. The word favorite means the best one out of many, so it is hard for me to narrow down one color choice, so I never do. I learned a lot about commitment as the word means committing to something my sister would say. "No, no, no according to Webster's dictionary the meaning of commitment is to pledge, vow, obligation, assurance, binder, promise, but I like dedication for my definition. As I think about whom I am, I think about being dedicated to a career in shoes because I see myself being loyal, devoted, and faithful to it. When I am dedicated to something, such as shoes I'm committed. I'm committed to school and graduating, I'm committed to going to college and becoming successful in my financial career, and I'm committed to shoes of color.

I guess style has a lot to do with fashion, but the way I see it you don't have to be a fashion stylist to love color. I am not a fashion stylist, and really don't want to be one, but I know a lot about color matching, and color combinations to coordinate outfits. I select the shoes first then I match them with to the outfit. That sound backwards, but if you understood how the brain works it makes perfect sense. Ok, I will admit that my favorite color choice is complicated. I prefer rose and all the colors that are created from the primary color of pink, but I have to like green because I was born with a green spot on the left side of my face. The medical professionals call it a birthmark, but I think it's an embarrassment to walk around with a green spot on my face. I used to ask God, five times a day… why me, why green, and why my face? Ever since I could interpret the English language I could hear people say, did you fall on your face sweetie, and I would always say, "NO IT'S A BIRTHMARK"! When I started school, kids would laugh at me insinuating that I got beat up in a fight. Everyone believed that because they always gave me their sympathy and apologizes for my bruised face. I guess that's why I have a high color IQ because I was born with two skin colors, brown and green. Colors have many different names today than before, and they all sound and look like ice cream flavors to me. There are over one hundred different names for color combinations that are all derived from the RGB *COLOR* model. This model shows additive colors of red, green, and blue light added together in various ways to reproduce a broad array of different colors. Luma is an interactive *COLOR* wheel that experiments with saturation, intensity, and hue. It corrects RGB for a measure of brightness, hue, saturation, lightness and perceptual color relationships. Hue is the correct word for pure spectrum *COLORS*. Any given *COLOR* can be described by its value and hue, or color tint. Saturation is determined by a combination of light intensity, and how much it is distributed across the spectrum of different wavelengths. To understand the different colors, and their names you must first know how color happens scientifically. Science is a subject that I pay close attention to because it will help me in the future of coordinating color combinations. I love looking at all the different colors, and the names of color fascinates me. The list is quite long but it's why I love color combinations, fashion, and shoes. I will be studying color mixing with a local artist that will give me private lessons on how to mix basic colors, which leads to more complicated techniques.

Color	Name	
	Alice Blue	
	Antique White	
	Aqua	
	Aquamarine	
	Azure	
	Beige	
	Bisque	
	Black	
	Blanched Almond	
	Blue	
	Blue Violet	
	Brown	
	Burly Wood	
	Cadet Blue	
	Chartreuse	

	Chocolate	
	Coral	
	Corn Flower Blue	
	Cornsilk	
	Crimson	
	Cyan	
	Dark Blue	
	Dark Cyan	
	Dark Goldenrod	
	Dark Gray / Dark Grey	
	Dark Green	
	Dark Khaki	
	Dark Magenta	
	Dark Olive Green	
	Dark Orange	
	Dark Orchid	
	Dark Red	
	Dark Salmon	
	Dark Sea Green	

	Dark Slate Blue	
	Dark Slate Gray	
	Dark Turquoise	
	Dark Violet	
	Deep Pink	
	Deep Sky Blue	
	Dim Gray / Dim Grey	
	Dodger Blue	
	Fire Brick	
	Floral White	
	Forest Green	
	Fuchsia	
	Gainsboro	
	Ghost White	
	Gold	
	Goldenrod	
	Gray / Grey	
	Green	
	Green Yellow	

	Honeydew	
	Hot Pink	
	Indian Red	
	Indigo	
	Ivory	
	Khaki	
	Lavender	
	Lavender Blush	
	Lawn Green	
	Lemon Chiffon	
	Light Blue	
	Light Coral	
	Light Cyan	
	Light Goldenrod Yellow	
	Light Green	
	Light Gray/ Light Grey	
	Light Pink	
	Light Salmon	
	Light Sea Green	

	Light Sky Blue	
	Light Slate Gray/Light Slate Grey	
	Light Steel Blue	
	Light Yellow	
	Lime	
	Lime Green	
	Linen	
	Magenta	
	Maroon	
	Medium Aquamarine	
	Medium Blue	
	Medium Orchid	
	Medium Purple	
	Medium Sea Green	
	Medium Slate Blue	
	Medium Spring Green	
	Medium Turquoise	
	Medium Violet Red	
	Midnight Blue	

	Mint Cream	
	Misty Rose	
	Moccasin	
	Navajo White	
	Navy	
	Old Lace	
	Olive	
	Olive Drab	
	Orange	
	Orange Red	
	Orchid	
	Pale Goldenrod	
	Pale Green	
	Pale Turquoise	
	Pale Violet Red	
	Papaya Whip	
	Peach Puff	
	Peru	
	Pink	

	Plum	
	Powder Blue	
	Purple	
	Red	
	Rosy Brown	
	Royal Blue	
	Saddle Brown	
	Salmon	
	Sandy Brown	
	Sea Green	
	Seashell	
	Sienna	
	Silver	
	Sky Blue	
	Slate Blue	
	Slate Gray / Slate Grey	
	Snow	
	Spring Green	
	Steel Blue	

	Tan	
	Teal	
	Tomato	
	Turquoise	
	Violet	
	Wheat	
	White	
	White Smoke	
	Yellow	
	Yellow Green	

I listed all of the colors because it's important to know how colors got their names. I took a babysitting training class so that I can get some experience, and be able to babysit on the weekends to earn money. I talked to five parents and they all asked, "What experience or training do you have?" At the time none, but I now have a certificate to prove I'm trained. I learned so much, like how to fold paper into a hot dog fold; that's the long way, or a hamburger fold that's the short way. Either way, you keep folding the paper in half until you get eight folds on both sides of the paper for the total of sixteen rectangles or squares however you see it. Next, we have fun with paint; every kid loves to play in paint because of the vibrant colors. We were told in training to really watch the younger kids as they will think the paint is ice cream at first until you tell them it's not. I pointed to my mouth at the same time telling the kids, "do not taste the paint please". Some painting tools I display are sponges; with or without handles, paint brushes, skinny or wide, long or short, or the index finger. I have ten colors to work with; light and dark blue, white, black, purple, yellow, orange, red, brown, and green, pink, all basic colors.

The goal is to show and teach the kids color mixing, and how to get more colors from the primary colors. I give everyone a dot of white paint using the hamburger folded paper, one color at a time to see if they are following directions, paying attention, and listening. If I don't have compliance in those three areas I have lost each kid's attention to complete the task. Then I will have to repeat the directions and check for compliance again, which is another set of rules. Some kids just don't get it, but I'm trained to exercise patience because kids are born either calm or with hyper tendencies. All of the calm kids are using one tool of their choice, and the hyper kids are out of seats running and jumping around the room. I have to teach behavior management while trying to teach art, and it slows the production time for others. After the kids mixed the first two colors I gave them the next two, and showed them a few colors on the chart so they will know what color they are trying to make. Working with five and six year olds is hard, but their fun and I could sure use an assistant. The kids that followed directions and did exactly what they were told to do received a reward at the end of class. A goody basket full of crayons, paints, colored pencils, stencils, and construction paper. I gave it to their parents, so the other kids will not see, and wonder why they didn't get a present. That's how the discriminating, separation, and labeling starts by making children feel unequal; I remember that feeling as a kid. As I become more experienced with mixing colors I'm thinking about a future in the shoe business, and how I will paint and decorate my store. I will use colors from the chart so my customers can see what colors are available in footwear. I will hire a shoe designer that can custom design shoes in a variety of color combinations. I don't like prints on shoes and solid colors is all you really need anyway. Animal prints get too complicated for me although many people love them. I can get a job for an online color advisor, or a columnist for a local or national newspaper to discuss shoe dilemmas. I will answer questions from people that want answers on fashion. Some people just don't know how to dress or coordinate colors, so mom always said if you don't know than ask somebody.

Black and Blue Colors…

Q. I've always been told never to wear black and navy blue together, but I've seen a lot of men wearing black shoes with dark navy blue pants. Is that acceptable dress or a fashion mistake?

My Answer…

A. Black and blue are perfectly OK to wear together, and actually the preferred combo especially for a man. I'm not sure exactly when or if the color combo became visually unappealing, but I would also use saddle brown and cordovan (a rich shade of burgundy and a dark shade of rose) because both colors are acceptable and great choices for navy.

The color chart gives me knowledge on how to answer questions about the fashion industry by keeping myself updated on the latest trends. Proving that this market is in demand by prompting women and men, girl and boys to keep trendy and dress to impress somebody. The outcome of such a demand in product and service equals financial success.

What to Wear…

Q. I have a psycho friend that jumps on everyone and anyone who wears grey and khaki together; particularly grey shirts, and khaki cargo pants. Is this a fashion no-no? My other question relates to shoes, can I wear black casual oxfords with blue jeans?

My Answer…

A. That's OK we all have friends that maybe a little different in their thought patterns. Grey and khaki is perfectly acceptable. In fact is a great combo especially if you are a guy, the two colors flow in lighter and darker hues. Black casual oxfords are perfectly OK for jeans but its better on a guy.

It will be hard sometimes to tell if the questions are coming from a male are female, but I can only give my best opinion and answer based on my color vision. I can offer a solution that solves a color or fashion issue. I understand that dressing and color matching is confusing, and many people develop stress and worry about what to wear for work, school, after 5, etc. I will be there to help them make a decision, keep them relaxed, and eliminate stress.

What to Wear…

Q. What is the proper fit and the proper way to wear tailored slacks? Looking at the length below the ankle, and the break at the top of your foot would be a good measurement. There is always a question about the fit around the waist. Where are slacks supposed to hang from, above or below the belly button?

My Answer…

The proper way to wear slacks is on the waist using the horizontal line from your belly button as a starting point.

This is a hard question for me because I don't know anything about slacks, and how they should fit. This person knows something about tailoring and how slacks should fit. I would need to know how big the waist is, I ask my seamstress for a general answer.

Mixing and Matching…

Q. I'm a terrible dresser. I have all these "nice" clothes in my closet, but when it comes to putting them together, I'm at a loss. Are there any websites that could help me, what could you recommend?

My Answer…

A. There are lots of fashion magazines and websites that you might find helpful, just look online or subscribe to outlet stores that will send you a sales booklet. Probably the best way to learn how to mix and match clothing is hands-on. I suggest the next time you go to the store you get a salesperson to help you put outfits together. If you buy clothing and accessories from one source it makes it easier to coordinate then you will get the hang of it. Sometimes the problem is in having too many clothes. I think people only wear about 20% of their wardrobe the rest just sits there taking up space, so try to work all your clothes in your weekly outfits by putting them together on Sunday. Dress up when you have no place to go, that's my motto.

Shoes For a White Suit…

Q. I own a white suit and I would like to know what color shoes to wear with it. I think I can probably wear white shoes too, can I or not, and if so where can I find them?

My Answer…

A. I think a light tan would be better. Usually during warm weather the best shoes to wear with a white suit are bucks, boat shoes, or hush puppies if you are a guy. For the ladies, they can go for low or high pumps just remember to add color whenever you wear white. However, any color will do so have fun selecting your shoes.

Never wear white after Labor Day mom always says, I don't know why because people do it anyway. Pretty much in this current era (2016) anything trendy goes before and after Labor Day. The Labor Day superstition on white clothing and accessories has been an etiquette sanctified rule since the nineteen twenties. I dare *NOT* to disobey this rule! A movie called, *Serial Mom*, punishes everyone for breaking the Labor Day rule. A psychopath murders people for wearing white in another movie. The average etiquette expert doesn't know how that rule came about, and can't explain it either. I hear a common explanation of being practical, but I still don't understand. For centuries, wearing white in the summer was a way of staying cool just like changing a dinner menu to lighter and cooler food choices form hot foods. Before air-conditioning existed people never walked around in T-shirts and halter tops as they do in today's society; they wore semi-formal clothing everywhere. Beating the heat has become fashionable in the twenty-first century. In the hot summer months white clothing kept New York fashion editors cool since that was, and still is, the place that starts fashion trends. Heavy rain in the fall made it a risk of getting white clothing wet and muddy. Vogue magazine would not tolerate the misconception of the color white, and set the tone for fashion. No White After Labor Day! This rule almost made a national holiday. There is never a functional reason to set a fashion rule, so fashion can break all the rules. Other historians speculate the origin of the, no white after Labor Day, rule may be symbolic. Here's why, in the twentieth century white was the uniform of choice for the Americans well to do, well off, or wealthy that escaped to warmer climates for months at a time. Light summer clothing provided a pleasing contrast to the dull urban life. Labor Day, is celebrated in the U.S. on the first Monday of September marking the traditional end of summer. Vacationers would stow their summer wares, and dust off their heavier dark-colored fall clothing. Labor Day is the official indicator that all the summer fun is over by going back at school, back to work, and back to doing whatever it is that's done in the fall. Of course the marketing industry promotes; it's time to reward yourself with a new fall wardrobe campaign. Whatever its origin, the Labor Day's rule is met with resistance from the fashion industry.

My Shoe Attraction

Social Media; Facebook, Twitter, Pinterest, Tumblr, Instagram, Viber, and the others is the new way of shoe shopping, not to mention shop sites, is a way ofshoe obsessing for me. Technology is a great outlet and tool used for both positive and negative reporting of news, and events about everything connecting us to shoes around the world. The history of communication told in many of my classes, dates back to 100 - 200 BC. Humans kept evolving by developing ways to communicate with others, we are now able to talk to everyone around the globe by learning each other's language, and using the internet. The first human messages for communication was sent out on foot and horseback. Papyrus rolls were made of dried reeds that became portable for writing in 500 BC. The Greeks started the first library for the world, I don't remember learning that or maybe I forgot, but humming pigeons were used to send out messages and return them back, in 776 BC. What smart little creatures pigeons are. So I found out that the very first postal service in China was developed in 900 BC, and the first encyclopedia was written in Syria, I always wondered who develop it. By 1775 the Greeks used a phonetic alphabet written from left to right. The Egyptians developed hieroglyphic writing in the same era that the Sumerians developed cuneiform writing. The alphabet replaced pictographs between 1700 and 1500 B.C. in the Sinitic world. I know someone will ask what is Sinitic, well what do you do when you don't know a word and the context clues are not helping…look it up! The current Hebrew alphabet became popular around 600 B.C. I said all that to say, it's important to know history because it explains why things occur today. The advancement of technology has really strengthened the process of communication, but humans are taking advantage of it. With social media I can make connections with so many people around the world it feels like I'm there. This form to communication bonds the human race together. The business world has its own unique way of communicating with people through advertisement.

I go to school on Saturday's for a rites of passage program to learn different things from what the public school teaches. The program prepares kids to live amongst the Wolfs. When I told my mom that she said; "that's right, living in this world you have to know personality types, and be able to recognize the types that supports who you are, and the ones that don't". We are learning to use communication through social networking to become a part of a media advertising project. This is a big opportunity for exposure to express our personal views and opinions about advertising. We are learning how to developed business ideas, and concepts that will help young adults learn how to become financially independent. I think this is great because with so many small and large businesses failing in the current state of the economy, what will my generation do for a job? It is also an opportunity to develop advertisement ads to market products and services to local and national companies. I love psychology because you can learn a lot about people, and it's a proven theory. Mom always tell me to stop trying to figure out people like my friends because you can't. They are too complicated, and if I go with that theory then I can't go wrong. Gardner's Theory of Multiple Intelligences proves there are seven levels of one's personality such as; bodily-kinesthetic, interpersonal-social, logical-mathematical, musical-rhythmic, verbal-linguistic, and visual-spatial. Knowing the personality types can predict how well people work together. In Saturday class the assignment is to create an ad for shoes by teams of three. We must follow a rubric for the project, and the winning team receives a reward. I like that we are motivated by teams to do our absolute best. We must first establish a team leader to manage our task, and make sure it looks good. I volunteered my leadership skills because I think I have the ability to lead the team. I was so excited that everyone agreed to advertise shoes per my suggestion. I love shoes so much I want to have a shoe house built just the old woman who lived in a shoe, she had so many shoes she didn't know what to do.

I told the team to bring in an old pair of pants and a new pair of shoes. "If you need to buy a new pair they don't have to expensive just something you can afford", I told the team. We developed an FYI (For Your Information) board for messages or notes to remind everyone why the project is so important. Most of my notes read; Reward: SHOES, SHOES, SHOES any pair you want at any cost! The idea of this project is to present a marketing ad to a buyer of a large department store featuring their shoe department. I told the team a little shoe history as we talked about what category of shoes to select. Everyone asked, what is the latest fashion in shoes, what's hot and what's not? They wanted to know what the celebrities are wearing. With that in mind we started researching and looking at different websites, we looked at E-news and other cable shows for shoes styles. This project required time and energy, and with so many other things to do in life I wondered if we could finish it by the due date. That meant working on the project during the week to be prepared for Saturday's class. I asked the team if they are ready for the daily commitment it's going to take to win.

Everyone including myself said yes, and from that point on the team met every day after school for the next two weeks. We helped each other with school work then worked on the project from five to ten o'clock pm. With social media, the internet, a printer, and all the supplies we needed for the project we are ready to go. I told the team members to wear their new shoes every Saturday to class. New shoes will give us the magic we need to win, simple as that. Before we knew it the deadline had approached, and we finished the project just in time. Yes! We are the first team to turn it the assignment.

We waited for six weeks to find out which team won. The director meet with companies, and negotiated a selling price, and terms for the advertisement ad. Our focus then shifted to other things like school work as it was that time of the year for state exams. I started thinking how much I love shoes as the project ended. It was hard work, but we had so much fun. I realized that shoes are my life, and I will confess that I do have a shoe fetish, but not in distorted way. I want to peruse a career in the shoe and fashion industry. I will admit that I am attracted to shoes, and I have a relationship with them for the long history of what footwear represents. The love of shoes came from not having a variety of them as a child. I enjoy looking at shoes online for hours wishing that I could buy every pair, and I enjoy going window shopping at the mall every chance I get. I like going to shoe stores just to smell the combination of leather, and other materials that smell like new shoes. Promoting and marketing shoes using a variety of strategies can make people go crazy by just glancing at a billboard or magazine ad. Shoe advertisement is associated with having a physical attraction to footwear. For me, shoes just mean picking out the right style and color for the right season, nothing more. During the project we reviewed movie clips that portrayed shoe fetishism for entertainment such as; *There's Something About Mary*, *While You Were Sleeping*, and *S__ In The City(I'm not allowed to say that three letter word)*. There are no filters for inappropriate advertisement in the American culture.

Today in Saturday school the team had a big surprise waiting. As soon I walked into the meeting room I saw three big boxes wrapped in real pretty paper. I thought they were stage props, but they wasn't. I figured the director will make an announcement about the boxes, but he didn't, in fact he keep us wondering for hours. Then finally he made an announcement that the winning team will receive the gift boxes. A manager first told everyone how well they did, and discussed the next step. The goal is to get an advertisement deal with a potential company as they review each team's ad. The teams were grouped by numbers then the manager spoke again announcing the winning team. Team #3 is this year's winner of the Advertisement award! Wow, as the team jumped for joy. The other teams came over and hugged us, and I felt a real sense of love from people who care. A box was handed to each one of us, and I didn't know what to expect inside. As we opened our boxes we started screaming because it was a gift card to Lord and Taylor's shoe department with no limited on what to spend on a pair of shoes. Hard work pays off and if it doesn't at least you tried. We gave the project our best creative work, and I was taught that you can only do the very best at whatever you do. The company treated all the teams to an exclusive shopping trip with a limo ride to the mall, I felt like a celebrity. We were escorted from the limousine to the shoe department as the local media was there for a news story; lights, camera, action! I was so excited about how I would react to a pair of dream shoes once they were on my feet. I don't want to embarrass myself by getting to happy because I don't have control sometimes over my shoe behavior, so I say a quick prayer for self-control.

I've already admitted that shoes are my life, and everything I do relates to researching, exploring, analyzing, and eye gazing at shoes. I take an art class at least once a year for further study, and to play around with color in many forms. The law of attraction is like a creative declaration, and one word affirmations describe a felling, or drive to do something that you are passionate about. Have you ever heard about a shoe tree? No, not shoes growing from a tree but a tree used as a symbol for recycling. Well, I think about all the litter that accumulates in any given place or form around the world; for example, the beach. The beach is not always left litter free from its many visitors in a given day. No one is perfect, but due try to pick up your belongings including the trash when leaving the beach. Imagine a local kid being offered a job to keep the environment clean by removing daily litter from the beaches. Kofi is a kid growing up in St. Croix, US Virgin Islands, he remembers riding in a car and seeing people throwing rash on the ground. For him that sight was disturbing, and he vowed to do something about it. Kofi would always yell out the window, "Stop littering, you are destroying the world". The environmental movement was slow to reach the small Caribbean Island, and they have a long way to go when it comes to recycling trash. Kofi has a passion for doing his part in keeping the environment clean, and clear of debris. The tourism and travel agency makes it a point to keep the beaches of St. Croix safe and clean. Tourism is the main attraction for the Islands beauty and natural wonders. The only way to keep visitors coming back is to keep the beaches safe, and maintain a clean environment. From all the beaches I've been to; Virginia Beach, South Beach, Myrtle Beach, Venice beach, Waikiki Beach, Labadi Beach in Ghana West Africa, beaches in Porto Rico, the beaches in Nausea Bahamas, Negril, Mammee Bay Beach, and Ocho Rios Beaches in Jamaica West Indies, andmany more. I've seen lots of food wrappings, bottles, cans, sandals, suntan location, cigarette butts, and tons of garbage. Garbage on the beach shouldn't exist at all!

During a spring break visit to St. Kitts and Nevis, another Caribbean Island, with my family we saw something so weird I laughed wondering… what that I'm looking at. I know it's a tree I could see that, but it had sandals, sneakers, and all kinds of footwear stuck to it. I found out it's an Island attraction called The Shoe Tree. A tree with a whole bunch shoes that were left on the beach and nailed to it. It's a way that local citizens get rid of the litter left behind. It certainly stands out for reasons that are unknown to tourist as we drove by the tree. The Island is known for its beauty, clean streets, and beaches. I took a picture of this wired shoe tree to make sure I show my friends, when I get back home, because they won't believe it. The shoe tree is a classy trashy tree! We asked a nearby local Islander what's the history of the tree and we were told; a gentleman who lived on the Island moved here from America, and called the beach his home, literally. Apparently after the big hurricane (Katarina) in Louisiana, the man lost everything and with nothing to lose he moved to St. Kitts. He's an electrician, and had an opportunity to get temporary work on the island. The man prayed he would find a long-term job that would keep him there. Eric, or the shoe man he's called, was on a mission to keep the beach clean hoping to impress local authorities by clearing trash, and recycling anything he can. Months after his arrival on the Island he fell in love with the beach, recycling, and a woman. This is where he wanted to be forever. Eric and his new love would often spend their free time searching the beaches for trash to recycle, but what they kept finding was sandals. Everyday Eric would find more sandals, which gave have him the idea of creating something for the visitor's to remember about the Island. With so many sandals collected Eric turned a lonely tree into a display of sandals, which is a symbol of many walks on the beach from people who came to visit St. Kitts, yet left a little piece of themselves behind. The shoe tree is now worth something to this Island, and it's the main attraction on the beach. Eric and his girlfriend collected eight hundred eleven shoes in one day, a record so far on a beach that is only a 200-meter stretch. With permission from the tourist bureau, Eric claimed a tree on a much traveled road along the beach side. He wanted to make sure all tourists and locals are able to see the shoe tree, which is in a perfect location to make his statement about recycling.

He added a universal recycling sign as the finishing touch that read, Do Not Litter on the Beach... Please! His statement about beach litter is a way of sending a clear message about his mission.

Eric worked for hours and climbed up the tree nailing down sandals until they were all hanging. That's how recycling became a daily ritual. People started leaving shoes at the base of the tree.

Day after day people continued leaving more and more shoes, and Eric started thinking about what will happen if he left the Island? Who will carry on the tradition of removing beach litter? Eric has more work than he asked for as he continues nailing more shoes on top of the old ones. The Visitor's Bureau made a deal with Eric by offering him a salary if he decides to stay on the Island. If he must go, they would save all the shoes found on the beach until his return. Eric returned to America, but he became an advocate and speaks to large and small audiences informing them about the importance of recycling. He always talk about the Shoe Tree in St. Kitts as a symbol of recycling, and his pride and joy. If you go to any beach around the world it's amazing how much garbage you'll find. Eric's mission and message is to recycle. The message in St. Kitts will spread to other Islands as Eric will inform Americans about keeping our beaches clean too. My message to the world as I stood on the beach tranquilized by its beauty, and hues of sea green is simple; we must all be responsible for protecting our planet earth.

A Shoe Sale

Many people live for a great shoe sale, and they are always searching for the fastest delivery service. I can only buy shoes when they are economically feasible; although online shopping have more options and sales, the local store is more convenient for me. Every time the word SALE is advertised mom goes crazy, and her energy level rises as she goes on a shoe mission. Mom attends any and all shoe sales, although she doesn't have money to buy all the shoes she love; she goes anyway just to look at the possibilities if she did. I always see a nice pair that I really, really want and I always feel sick to the stomach because I can't have them. This method mom created is to teach *La-La* and I the concept of managing money by not getting everything we want just because it's on sale. I don't understand why mom takes us with her to shoe sales when we are not buying because we have no money, it's to torture. When money is available we can buy at least one pair of footwear. So I check some of my favorite websites to see what's on sale, I always find a pair within my budget. Some online stores advertise for sales everyday just to keep consumers looking, and that's a way to lure us in. I think it's a good plan, but if I managed or owned a shoe store I would only advertise a sale once or twice a month. There are consignment shops that allow people to sell their shoes and other items; you get paid once the item sells. There are nice shoes to be found in this type of store if you don't mine recycled shoes. EBay is my favorite website for shoe shopping, its open 24 hours/7 days a week, and have every shoe I can imagine on sale. My cousin (Nia) is going to college for visual communications, and she is helping me with ideas for designing my fabulous shoe store, I'm seriously considering a shoe store business more and more for a career. I can start planning early by collecting ideas in a scrapbook and blog, I can also redesign my closet using an organizational strategy. I haven't researched yet, but I need to look into wholesale pricing where I can buy all type of shoes. How much profit I will make in order to see money grow, that's what I want to know. All businesses have a marketing plan to promote sales its part of advertising and business strategy to sell merchandise. I'm sure sale items are carefully priced to make a profit, so I believe a sale is not really a sale at all. A business will not risk losing money for consumers to save money.

Mom already knows that I will not buy used shoes at a garage sale on Saturday mornings. Mom always get me up on Saturday's and drag me along with her to a garage sale. I always tell mom NO, I don't want to go. I'm always in a good shoe dream when I'm suddenly awaken with a request for me up to get up. Garage sales have lots of things to buy that mom can use around the house. Of course I always glance at the shoe collection that sells for a dollar or two a pair, anything above that should be new shoes. I waited in the car this time then I see shoes in moms hand as she walks up to the car. I don't want to look at her, so I start shaking my head and say "NO, NO, and NO", I don't want them. Mom begs me to take a look at a new pair of shoes that sparkles and glows. To my surprise that pair of shoes is new and cost $10.00, which is way more than what I would ever pay for a pair of shoes from a garage sale. There is nothing wrong with looking at shoes that appears in a garage sale. That's what we do at a real shoe store anyway. The shoes are green, my second favorite color, but a different kind of green. The color green that reminds me of pistachios… yum, yum. I didn't want to break my own shoe rules, so I didn't want buy them for that reason. Mom said I need to reconsider getting the shoes. Nia is graduating and the shoes match the color of a dress I have. This decision felt like either the biggest mistake of my life, or a chance of a lifetime. Honestly, I had a feeling about those shoes because I dreamt about them. I need to call my grandma because she will tell me exactly what to do in this kind of dilemma. First of all, my grandma brought me a beautiful green dress, and I can't take on the previous troubles of those shoes. Because the shoes are new and never worn it is ok to buy them. When I call my grandma she always give me good advice because she understands my love for shoes, and she listens to me. Grandma knows what to do when I get myself into sticky situations, but what she doesn't know is my shoe rules. Grandma said, "Get the shoes and get them quick, especially if they match the dress". The color would be hard to find and then I would have to wear a black or white shoe, the two colors I despise. OK it's time to decide, the lady told us the shoes were never worn, which means they are brand new, "Let's get them" I said. I can't wait to get home to see how well the shoes matches the dress. I thanked mom and grandma for making my dream come true today. I appreciate the little things my family does to make me feel special.

My aunt is planning a moving sale, but she's not really moving it just sounds better than saying garage sale. Either way I will be making signs to advertise the sale. The items will be a combination of everyone's stuff including five boxes of donated shoes from an aunt that recently passed away. My aunt had over three hundred pairs of shoes in her shoe inventory. I could only imagine what her closet was like, probably one of the best design closets to accommodate all of her shoes. I volunteered to help sell, only shoes, at the moving sale, and will be my first job as a sales associate; I'm getting paid too. I spent the rest of the day helping and organizing the garage, I was excited about that! My aunt's shoes are fabulous and many of them look brand new as if she only worn them once. The only problem is her shoe size I which my foot was an eight like hers, but I wear a size nine. If I was considering buying a pair, which I WAS NOT, they are too small. There were plenty of shoes with many colors and styles, so I grouped them by size to make it easier to sell. I looked in my closet to see what I can add to the moving sale inventory, and I do have a few things to add along with mom and *La-La*. ay was I donating any of my shoes as mom suggest. Today is the day for the moving sale and we are open for business, the weather is perfect.

As I was getting bags out of mom's car the first customer arrives, so I hurried back to make a shoe sale. I made more signs to bring some attention to the many shoes I really want to sell. My aunt said I should sell them all for the same price, but she doesn't know anything about selling used shoes. Some of the shoes are worth more than others, and I counted a total of three hundred sixty pair of footwear that I must sell. I started pricing at three dollars and I went up to ten dollars on the more expensive, and hardly worn shoes. My first sale was a lady with her daughters buying six pairs of shoes. I'm excited as I put the shoes in a bag, but noticed I sold a pair of my own shoes. I froze, going in and out of shock with disbelief, the lady asked if everything is OK, when tears started streaming down my face. I said," one moment please" and ran inside the house with the bag in my hand looking for mom. "Mom, what are my shoes doing at the garage sale?" She said, "I don't know". I looked at her and knew she was not telling the truth. I know she took them out of my closet because I have an inventory of my shoes, and I did not take a pair out for the moving sale. Mom wanted me to get rid of those particular shoes because she doesn't like them, nor does she like my attitude when I wear them. I believe mom was trying to trick me to believe I wanted to sell them by taking them out of my closet, or having me question myself; maybe I left them by the door by mistake. I always practice putting my shoes in my closet when I take them off, never leaving them anywhere but where they belong, so I know where they are. I had to make a decision, so I'm thinking... OMG what should I do, the people are waiting. I don't want to miss eighteen dollars, so I ran outside and finished the sale as I continued to smile and excused myself for the delay. I sold the shoes because it was the right thing to do. The moving sale made a huge profit as I sold out of shoes. Although I was upset at mom she taught me a lesson about giving to others that are less fortunate. I'm glad I was able to help that lady who needed shoes for her daughters. I brought a new pair that replaced the ones I sold, so when you give you also receive that's Karma. Look it up!

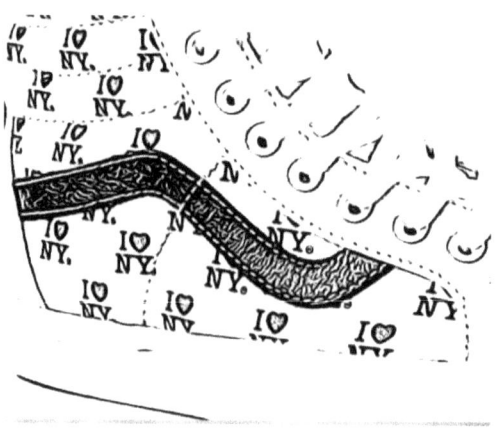

I use to visit my aunt once a year in New York City; Lights, Camera, Action! Although my aunt has passed on, I will never forget her shoe collection. Her closet is much larger than my small one, and was very organized by putting everything including her shoes back in its place, and quoted, "There is a place for everything". I believe when you create a space for your things it becomes a home. I wish I had my aunt's foot size because if I did, what a shoe collection I would have. *Dee* had a passion for shoes; I think it runs in my family. My aunt always had a pair of new shoes waiting upon my arrival, she knew my style and understood my passion too. I'm learning about closet design and creating a masterpiece with limited working space. Her shoes was organized by the most expensive to the least, and had an attractive layout plan on her closet. When I go into the city (Manhattan) my aunt took me uptown, downtown, crosstown, Harlem the upper and lower Eastside, then we would end the day with a walk in Central Park. I Love New York! That's what my T-shirt reads, I wear it each time I'm in New York. The city has so many options for shoes, places to buy them, and one big sale. Most of the shoes are imported from around the world, and available in one place. Italy is the number one place for leather shoes and accessories that are available in New York. I am so lucky to buy leather shoes every time I'm in New York. Sandals are the best for summer time because they help me walk faster and stand taller. I look for the best sales before buying just to make sure it's the best deal. My aunt knew exactly where to go, Delancey Street is a shoppers market both retail and wholesale. I remember, getting real excited about the possibilities of what store to go in first when I was there. With so many stores and sale signs everywhere it's impossible to visit every store in one day, so I had to make a choice, and I made it quick. I selected three stores by looking in the windows first, then I made my decision. The first store has the best options and deals for me, so that's where I brought my leather sandals. There is so much involved in buying a pair of shoes, first I have to feel, touch, and then smell the leather first. Because of my love for shoes I can sense a connection between my feet and the ground. I'm adding more shoes to my collection this year, and that's good news for me.

I have a great idea for a school fundraiser that I need to discuss with my principal since I'm on the student council committee. This is my first time being a part of a school committee, and I can actually share my ideas with people for team building. I presented the idea for a fundraiser to the committee, and if they agree we will present it to the student body. The big idea is to promote a fundraiser to collect shoes, old and new. After the moving sale I thought this would be a great community and school event. We will ask students and parents to donate shoes they no longer wear, it's that easy! The funds will go towards a school trip for summer break. The committee will send out flyers to advertise the shoe drive with a goal to collect three thousand pairs. If we could pull this off we can sponsor another fundraiser soliciting local businesses; raising even more money for the trip. It would be nice to travel overseas to a middle school and give away shoes. It's real important for the committee to make sure all the planning is coordinated and organized for a successful fundraiser. We came up with a great flyer, and got it approved by the principal to start. The Fundraiser will end in May, a month before school ends giving the committee seven months to raise money. All grade levels; six, seventh, and eighth will participate giving everyone an opportunity to attend the field trip. This fundraising effort is a two part project to raise enough money for all students to attend by paying something they can afford (a low fee). The first set of flyers went out to all schools in the district, which includes fourteen elementary, four middle, and two high schools along with a child developmental center, and a state of the art technology career center. We need all the shoes we can get to plan for part-two of this fundraiser. The committee decorated fifty oversize boxes; one per school that will be placed in the foyer on each campus. A special recognition will be given to the campus that collects the most shoes for the fundraiser. Once a week after school, a teacher will drive the district van, or bus, to collect shoes from each campus. This project takes a lot of work and energy; it's a job without a paycheck, but the effort and experience will be worth it at the end. The committee normally meets once a month, but when an event is planned we agreed to meet when necessary. I'm wearing the same pair of shoes to every committee meetings just for luck.

Now that the first part of the fundraising has begun the team must start planning for part- two. First we must talk about ideas for the summer trip. Everyone gave their input about where we should travel, but we don't know how much money we will raise for a total cost. Where can we go is the big question everyone is asking as if they never been out of the country before, and scared to go. "We should travel overseas" I said, or just a local trip might be ideal for some kids. I'm thinking big… someone replies, "Not enough time or money to plan a trip out of this country, let's just stick to a local journey". I agree although I think we can at least talk about a possibility of an overseas trip, and I tell them why. "Many villages around the world work together to meet the basic needs as a group, and footwear is something they really, really need. What if we can actually take or even send shoes to a village in Africa?" I tell the committee a story about my father being an African man, and living in the village today. I continue, "Things we consider necessities are things they don't have. Things like a toothbrush, toilet paper, soap, food, and yes shoes". We continued to talk about the part-two of the fundraiser, which is to contact small businesses in and out of the local community to inform them of the current fundraiser. We send a text message first then followed it up with a letter asking of a monitory donation that would go towards our field trip. I give them a bigger picture of our goal and purpose, to travel overseas this summer and deliver shoes to children living in villages. Although the team has not made a final plan it was a good pitch. I followed up for the conversation, per their request, by writing a proposal that outlines the goal, purpose, and details of the fundraiser. The team collaborated with fifty local businesses as they all sounded pretty upbeat, and willing to make a financial contribution. All donations will be mailed directly to the school. As the deadline approached for the shoe collection there are thousands of shoes piled up in an empty room at school, and all I could see was dollar signs in my eyes. The committee made an announcement for volunteers to help count all those shoes we collected, while the other members opened envelops that hopefully had money in them. After we counted all the shoes it was way over our goal, with a final count of fifty thousand pairs. WOW, the committee received fifty thousand dollars in donations from businesses too. The team can at least start thinking about a possibility of an overseas trip, but it will all depend on the money from the shoe sale.

As we now prepare for the actual fundraiser, the shoe sale, the school is getting ready for the biggest sale ever. It's been the talk around school and town for the past five months with lots of positive energy behind it. No final plans for the summer trip yet because we need to see the profit gains after the sale. The team and volunteers spend Friday night, and all day Saturday preparing a week in advance for this event. Everyone made signs that were real creative and colorful that will be placed around the community for advertising. I gave a speech on selling strategies, and how to promote and close a shoe deal. I answered questions, gave tips, advice, and told everyone to wear a pair of magic shoes for this fundraiser. Flyers were passed out to all the homes in and out of the school district, and public service announcements were made on all the local radio stations. Today is a good day for the biggest fundraiser of my life, and I'm real nervous about it. The team and volunteers arrived at the school an hour before starting time to pray for a successful day. The shoe sale was setup outside of the school, and we stayed busy from sun up to sunset until every pair was sold. We did it… AMAZING! We are up all night counting money, then shocked when the final amount was announced. Two hundred fifty thousand dollars, and this is what the numbers look like in the numerical version, $250,000.00. I've never seen so much money at one time, so I'm excited! Next week, more planning and decision making for the committee to finalize the summer trip. The principals met with the team and expressed their gratitude for our effort, time, and commitment to the school and the community; we are awarded with a ribbon of excellence. Instead of giving half the money to the school the committee was allowed to keep all of it to help with expenses for all students to attend. It felt so good when everyone gave me a hug and said, "You are so talented, and smart to have organized such a big event". All I could do is smile, and say, "Thank You"! I can't take all the credit, it was a team effort as they listened to my ideas and supported the project. Although a few people thought we should do something different instead of going to Africa; they all came together at the end and thought what an experience it will be.

It's going to be a great opportunity for the students to give students in Africa things they need for school, shoes and school supplies, yes clothes too. The team talked more about how American kids are not in touch with reality. The reality of being privileged, and how they don't appreciate what they have verses what other kids in Africa live without. This field trip will help American kids give more and want less. When the district gave our school approval to travel overseas I was shocked once again, knowing they would say, Not Approved. This is going to be a real life adventure for some kids. First, a formal letter will be sent to all parents outlining the trip itinerary, and the conditions required to travel. Such as; a passport, visa, shots, and a small fee for every student to cover other expenses that includes airfare, hotel, food, transportation, and tours. For every student that signs up to go they will bring a new or old pair of shoes for a student in the village school. Our middle school attendance is six hundred students for; 6th, 7th, 8th grades combined. If everyone wants to go on the trip we will be short of money, so that's why a small fee will be required. The parent's letter has a due date to respond with a yes or no answer, and a deposit of the total fee, so the team can move forward with planning the trip. The airline will give us a huge discount according to the number of students we have. I researched hotels, tour companies, restaurants, buses for transportation, and thought about paying my dad handle all the details on the ground. He will be our tour guide as he agreed on a reasonable fee. I sent him a list of all the services we'll need, so he can send me an itemized itinerary for our budget. We received three hundred eleven replies from parents that wanted to sign up. WOW, that's a big number but not as big as six hundred, so it will be a lot easier to manage that group size I think. OK we need chaperons and lots of them, and I wonder if we will really get three hundred eleven students to go. We will see when the letters go out about final payments due of five hundred dollars. The deadline approached, and we are back at the meeting table, we received two hundred eighty five payments and we may get a few late payments too. The date for the summer trip to West Africa was set, we sent out letters with more information and a timeline for passports and other necessary fees, including a list of what to do, and what to bring. The total number of participants is two hundred ninety-four including parent and teacher chaperones.

We will be flying into the city of Accra, Country of Ghana, West Africa via Delta Airlines out of JFK International Airport. The committee gave everyone a book on Ghana to study along with an itinerary of the trip for the next seven days outlining tours, hotel room assignment, group assignment, and other information of stuff to do. Everyone arrived at the airport on time, excited and ready to go. I am so happy my sister was able to take this trip back home to Africa with me, something we always do together. Eleven long hours in the air, so glad it's a direct flight. All I want to do is sleep after dinner is served, then I told my sister to wake me up when we get there. I did wake up twice to use the bathroom, and when I woke up again we were landing. Landing in Accra is a feeling I cannot describe. Everyone is hyped as we make our way off the plane. I have never traveled in such a group before; everyone wore yellow tee shirts with USA and the name of our school on the back. We made our way to the buses after the long customs check in, and took a short ride to the hotel. For the next seven days we will experience Africa like never before; although I've been here many times before, it's my first home, it's where I belong. My father is from a village outside of Accra in a city called Kumasi. I have an aunt that lives and work in Accra, she will meet us at the airport with dad. Samy is her name, and she has a teachers store in the first mall of Accra; we are planning a visit her on a trip to the mall. I must see what type of shoe stores they have, and maybe buy a pair or two. The village trip is scheduled for tomorrow, and dad will speak to the whole group in the morning during breakfast giving highlights of the tour. Morning came quickly, and everyone seems jet lagged because they are moving real slow. We collected everyone's shoes they brought, which filled one small bus alone. After breakfast and a briefing everyone boarded the other ten buses for the trip to dad's village, it will take four maybe five hours to get there. As I look around on my bus I see everyone asleep, so I take a nap too. We are finally here and the entire village is waiting for our arrival. Upon entering the village we see Ghana and US flags, and beautiful colors of traditional clothing for miles. The Americans are coming, that's all I could think about at the moment; I feel like a celebrity again. As we are getting off the bus everyone waves as we are escorted to the school for a tour. We walked around as the tour guide (dad) explains the structure and details of living in a village. Then we met the chief (every village in Africa has a Chief), and the men, women, and children of the village including my family. As everyone clapped and cheered; I started crying because I was real nervous. My teacher gave a speech to the village about how I organized a school fundraiser that led us here to my family's village. She went on to say how American students are committed to giving, and the students brought everyone a gift. When everyone in the village including the students they started dancing, playing drums, and chanted what sounds like revival songs. We celebrated by eating lunch that the village prepared for us, which is a traditional meal, and very tasty as always. The students gave everyone a beaded bracelet as a gift, and I will add this one to my collection. Hours later we were back on the bus, back at the hotel as we continued the rest of the week touring every inch of the city and nearby areas; eating, dancing with the drummers, celebrating, and having a good time. We also went to the mall to visit my aunt and of course I had to buy a pair of shoes, but I won't put them on my feet for reasons I can't explain yet. Time goes by quickly because before we knew it, it was time to get back on the bus heading to the airport. It was great being back home, and seeing my dad and aunt. I keep seeing a smile on everyone face, which meant everyone enjoyed themselves.

Next year I will join student council again and organize a trip for the village students to come to America, and call it an exchange project (if everyone agrees). Where did the summer go, it's time for school already another month please. Everyone is talking about the summer trip, and the kids that didn't go regret they missed out. The team is begging me to plan another trip, so I didn't have to ask, and now I'm Ms. Popular. I don't want to take all the credit again, but everyone keeps asking me to come up with an idea as if they couldn't? "Let us all put an idea on the table and vote on it", I said. And so they did… but I was still voted the winner! OK fine, I pitched my idea of inviting the village students to America, and helping them fundraise to get here.

We can match what they come up with, or ask their government to sponsor the trip to America, simple. I was really insisting on keeping the shoe theme because shoes make everyone happy. What we can do is, help the African students plan a shoe shopping spree in New York. Our school did the same type of fundraiser this school year, but a clothes drive instead of shoes. The team didn't collect as many clothes as shoes, but twenty thousand pieces is a good number for the sale. We received twenty thousand in cash donations, so the numbers are down, but we sold all the clothing. Everyone was excited as the reward this time will be only a select number of students that will travel to New York, and escort the African group on tour. With only fifty students from Africa that are planning to travel will keep the cost down, and make planning a lot easier. My aunt and father helped the students in the village organize the fundraiser with the government paying for the airline tickets, as our school gave a cash donation from the fundraiser, so it all worked out financially. The school committee gave a writing contest that included a power point presentation, and a visual display of the student's interpretation of how they would organize, and plan the summer trip to New York. Only fifty winners will be chosen based on meeting the criteria for the contest. Unfortunately only forty students qualified to go. The thought of another rewarding summer of kids helping each another is a step in the right direction for a better world.

The last day of school has finally arrived, hello summer! The students from Ghana arrived in New York for the first time on American soil, as our team coordinated the same arrival time to meet up at JFK International Airport. Everyone stayed at the same hotel in Manhattan close to the shopping district. I told dad to send African garments for everyone on the tour as gifts for the American students. We will give the exchange students beaded bracelets our team personally made from materials we brought in Ghana. During the five day visit to New York a shopping trip was planned to buy shoes, and other items they wanted. We toured the hot spots of New York City and the surrounding borrows, and did all the typical American things that teenagers do; glued to a cell phone, mall, movies, fast food, paintball, arcade, dancing, amusement park, subway ride, and having fun!. We give them a true experience of the American life. New York is a great American experience, and all the students keep saying they are having so much FUN! I'm so glad dad was able to come because I miss him a whole lot. A party was planned and everyone wore new clothes, and of course shoes. The energy in the building was off the roof (high), everyone was so full of life and couldn't stop dancing. A celebrity rapper appeared at the door, and everyone went crazy! We took pictures, got autographs on our hands, arms, and sneakers. Before the African students went back home we made a commitment to stay in touch, and so we did.

A Shoe Closet

Every young girl and maybe boy, dreams about having the coolest closet filled to the ceiling with shoes, clothes, and accessories for all occasions. The average closet is never big enough to hold all the clothes that accumulated over time, not to mention shoes. I like to keep all my shoes and wear them until the soles fall off, so that I can have a variety to select from. I've saved over 30 pairs of shoes, but with limited closet space I often find myself searching high and low to find the right pair to wear. One day I hope to have a closet like my aunt's or grandma's, they have plenty space to hold 100 pairs of shoes. My sister and I share a small closet and I can barely fit my foot in. Our closet always looks a mess because clothes have no room to breathe. Of course, everything can not fit in this box has no space for our clothes, so we just stuff everything in. I can't wait for the day when we have a bigger house with large closet spaces.

A custom built closet is a must have when you're in love with fashion and shoes. I'm learning there is a hefty price to pay for organization, renovation, and remolding of a shoe closet. I will start organizing my closet by taking everything out first. Then measure the closet in square feet. This training will help me think of ideas to manage a shoe store, but I must learn to work with the space I have instead of complaining about it. Mom always said, appreciate what you have instead of complaining about what you don't have. Celebrities do have the best organized closets because they need plenty of room to store all the clothes, shoes, accessories they buy. I took the liberty of studying the layout of my grandma's and aunt's closet. I brought my sketch book to write down ideas of what I would like my closet to model. Everyone, for the most part, wants their closet to be organized. Whether it's by size, style, or color people want to walk into the closet and scan what to wear instantly. By not feeling like a hurricane just past threw and so you panic. I started my home renovations with all the closets first for experience on designing closets in general. Everything comes out of the closets first, then I measure the walls and floor space. Since *La-La* and I share space, its necessary to let her choose what side she wants first. She is my big sis, respect your elders. We also agreed on closet rules, colors, and must haves. I got rid of all the junk, things that don't belong, and clothes that are too small, to big, to faded, or no longer a fashion statement. I created a shoe rack out of the boxes they came in. I used crates for the extra space to put things in then made shelves for an organized look. I want to be creative with my closet to impress my mom and *La-La,* with my skills.

Now that some of the hard work is done, I'm ready for the fun part, decorating! Another way to make the closet look fun is to make with a shoe collage that covers the entire wall. Good thing I've been saving magazines since I was six, mom lets me do a little hording. I will turn my closet into one big shoe masterpiece. I asked my sister to help because half of the closet is hers, which makes her responsible and gives us something to do on a boring Saturday morning. I made sure we had enough magazines, so I collected more. We cut out every shoe we found out of one hundred magazines until our hands begged us to stop.13 I think it's safe to estimate 2,000 pictures of footwear. We chose my sister's favorite color, coral for the uncovered walls in the closet. We spent the whole night painting before starting the wall collage. This project is bigger than what I expected, so we will probably finish on Sunday. I was up early Sunday morning to get started and finish the closet, I hope. In no order, I hung up shoes all over the wall until they were everywhere, I went shoe crazy! When La-La gets up she will help me finish the collage and put everything back in the closet. The closet renovation project is finally over, we took a step back and marveled over our work. Our closet looks magnificent! After showing mom what we have been doing for the past two days. After looking at remodeled closets online I realize that there are so many fascinating images of closets, I compare options when looking at closet space first. And always consider the space of the closet

I read an article on popular children's books and the top books purchased. The book, "Beyonce's Big Tall Shoes", (no not the celebrity Beyonce Knowles), shows a closet full of pumps in all colors. Beyonce always wanted to wear her mother's shoes and loved her crocodile pumps, her summer sandals, and all her lace up strappy pumps. One day she was allowed to wear any pair of shoes she wanted. Beyonce felt beautiful, she felt glamorous, and she felt like a celebrity. It didn't take long before Beyonce realized she couldn't do all her usual activities in heels, so now she appreciates her bare feet. Her mother's shoe closet is like no other, and the shoe display in the book was amazing to see. If magic was real, and it's not, I would try on all the shoes on display and think about what each pair would do on my feet. I match shoes with my clothes and its always color combinations and hues. When it's cold outside a pair of boots are used to warm my feet. If I wear a skirt, a pair of peep-toes or sling-backs will do, or maybe a pair of elegant black pumps will do.

A shoe closet has a life of its own and when I look at other closets it allows me to envision a masterpiece. I love to explore my creative world through meditation that allow me to focus. One day I will have an opportunity to design a shoe store of my own. I enjoy pretending and playing make believe as a way of having mental fun. I begin by using my imagination with an idea of a closet system for the shoe store. The Closet Shoe Store is the official name for my business. The actual store will measure 1,035-square-foot (96-square-meter), and when customers come inside they will be amazed to see that the store resembles a real closet. With wall to wall shelves from top to bottom and shoe racks offering a variety of footwear and accessories. Mirrors in the fitting rooms will cover all the walls giving a back view, and open rooms for customers to request help when needed. Restroom stalls will be glamorously decorated and clean with a good smelling scent. Most closets have hanging space with no shelving or drawers, so I added this in the layout design. When remodeling a closet, maximizing available hanging space is important by incorporating double hanging areas. The

Closet Shoe Store will sell apparel, accessories, footwear, and everything you would normally see in a closet. For long hanging items such as dresses, a closet pole about 60-70 inches off the ground will be used for the extra space. The shelves will hold items to grab and go, allowing more room for displays. The Closet Shoe Store is based on the Feng Shui concept of open space for movement to enhance balance in the environment. The clothing and accessories will be accessible towards the front of the closet. This will lead customers to hidden areas in the store. It's a good idea to leave at least 36 inches between the ceiling and top closet shelves. This way you will have at least a foot of storage space above the closet systems for storing small boxes, folded Items, seasonal stuff, bags miscellaneous things. I would use small closet items for the store's décor and items to fit the occasion. I am including a few modular units that will mount on the wall without touching the floor. This will really give the store a custom closet look and feel for customers to shop with ease. Deep drawers will give more space for stocking and storing merchandise. This closet system will help customers to see everything when they walk into the Closet Shoe Store. Smaller items like socks, undergarments, scarfs; I will add a see-through slide-out baskets or bins in a wall unit. Closet systems can make the day-to-day functions of dressing easier and less stressful. Just for the fun of it I will add a small space in The Closet Shoe Store for a coffee bar with a few round tables, chairs, and Wi-Fi.

I enjoy themes in small room closets because I can be real creative using my imagination. In many homes small storage areas becomes junk spaces by putting everything inside with no direction. A perfect way to give clothes and shoes the freedom they need (in a closet system) is to be noticed by the owner/customer for a quick pick up. Turning small rooms into a useful organized space for a purpose is ideal. When I plan a closet design I think of a realistic need for that space, maybe a hidden office or an area for toys. For the closet store project, I will install a counter that will act as a desk for a computer system, making sure it's the right height for legs to fit underneath. Above the desk can be floating shelves for office supplies, and other needs. I will paint the interior white or an accent color. Then add framed photos on the wall for a homey touch, and use the inside of the door for a bulletin board; that sounds pretty cool right? Then tuck a stool under the counter, or use a small desk chair. How about an entertainment center in your room for the TV, but no wall space for it; the closet is a great place for that too. I can replace the swinging door with a sliding pocket door, which will be easy to move the TV around. I How about hanging baskets to add storage for remote controls, and other things related to the TV. Without knowing the layout of a room I have to make sure the closet serves its purpose. A craft closet or sewing space is another idea to keep all craft supplies in one place. Remove the clothing rod in a closet, add wallpaper or paint and give the walls a decorative look. I've seen extended closets become a whole room. When customers walk into the Shoe Closet Store, they will be surprised of what they may find.

I will show you a few unusual types of canvas sneakers if that's what you like. With so many ways to create art on canvas I came up with twenty-six styles that I can feature in The Closet Shoe Store. Then advertise every six months a new design on canvas sneakers, for a store display. The designer will be at the grand opening.

All-Over Stripes - Cover your shoes in stripes with half-inch wide masking tape, leaving space in between the rows of tape. Take your shoes outside and spray paint them. Let the paint dry then pull off the tape and you've got stripes!

Faux Tie-Dye - Soak your shoes in water so they're pretty waterlogged, use water based magic markers to draw solid shapes of different sizes and colors on the wet canvas. The ink shapes will bleed around the wet fabric and overlap in spots, giving the illusion of tie dye. Think about what happens when you drop food coloring in water, it's the same effect. Let the shoes dry completely then spray them with a clear adhesive spray.

RIGHT/LEFT - Using the directions on a package of iron-on lettering from a craft store, iron the words "Right" and "Left" on the front of each sneaker. Stuff the shoes with newspaper first to make the shoes stiff enough to iron. Try a different combination of words (short enough to fit on your sneaker): IN/LOVE, US/THEM, FOR/SURE, Or whatever you want.

Golden Shoes - Stuff the inside of your shoes with newspaper to protect them; then spray your shoes with gold spray paint.

Splatter Paint - Dye your shoes in a washing machine or sink with fabric dye. Follow the directions on the package. Dip a toothbrush in acrylic paint and pull back the bristles to splatter paint all over your shoes. Splatter from different angles, or get a splatter tool for a better technique.

Broken Heart - Cut the shape of a heart out of scrap fabric. Then cut a zigzag shape down the middle of the heart so it looks like it's been cracked open. Hot glue one half of the heart on each shoe.

Boat Shoes - Glue nautical themed ribbon around the opening of your shoes. Then hot-glue or iron-on nautical patches to the front of each shoe. Ahoy!

Chained - To attach chains to the front of each shoe use safety pins, and make sure that the clasp closes under the tongue of your shoe. You can use old broken necklaces, or find chains at a hardware store.

Polka Party - Cover your shoes in tiny polka dots by dotting the tip of a sharpie/fine point permanent marker all over your shoes. Try these color palettes: Analogous colors (colors that are side by side on the color wheel) such as blue, turquoise, and green. Complimentary colors (colors that look the brightest when they're next to each other) such as purple and yellow; or instead of using color go with the subtle approach with different shades of gray and black

Shark Shoes - With a washable magic marker or erasable pen, outline triangles around the rubber-sole of your slip-on shoes. Use the triangles as a guide to fill in all the empty spaces on the rubber sole with black acrylic paint (or you could use a permanent black marker). Then paint two angry eyes on top of your shoes.

On The Fringe - Use a zig zag design, then trim and start at the back of the shoe and work your way around both sides ending in the back at the starting point with hot-glue. Use leather, suede, or pleather fringe around the top edge at the opening of the shoe.

Stencil Collage - Use masking tape to secure stencils all over your shoes. Cover empty spaces with tape to prevent being painted. Then take the shoes outside and spray the stencil areas with paint.

Weather URL - When using fabric paint, draw a rain cloud on one shoe and a sun on the other.

Foot Notes - Grab your box of love notes, favorite book of poetry, or English Literature textbook then copy the text on your sneaker with a sharpie/fine point permanent marker. Write each line at a different angle so the text looks jumbled like notes on a sketchbook. If you start writing a line and it doesn't fit on the shoe don't force it. Just stop mid-sentence and start up again somewhere else.

Fake Laces - Hot glue two pieces of thin ribbon ("X" shapes) across the front of each shoe. Then glue on two long pieces to tie in a bow above the "X" to create shoelaces. Don't forget to keep your shoes tied!

Rhinestone Heart - Create a big white heart on the front of each sneaker using rhinestones.

Big Bow - Hot glue a big bow to the heel of each sneaker. Be sure to put a dab of glue in the knot of the bow to keep it tied.

Hermes (Olympian Greek God) Shoes - Hot glue long thin feathers around the curves of your shoes so they look like wings on your feet just like the messenger of the Gods!

Like a Rhinestone Cowgirl - Hot glue rhinestones along the seams of your shoes without any space in between each rhinestones.

Fragrant Feet - Paste hot glue to the bloom of a fake flower to the front of each shoe then spray the flower with flowery perfume to make it fragrant!

Tip Toe Through the Tulips - Hot glue pieces of felt shaped like tulips, flower stems, and leaves to the front of each of shoe.

All That Glitters Is - Brush silver glitter glue all over your shoes. The glue will dry clear and your shoes will be super sparkly.

Spiked - Attach studs and spikes with hot glue (you can usually find them at any craft) to the tongues of your shoes.

Charmed - Use safety pins to attach charms from key chains or broken jewelry to the tongues of your shoes.

Shoe Magic

I will always remember Dorothy from the Wizard of Oz. I love those sparkly ruby red shoes she wore because they were indeed magical. Once Dorothy put on her shoes she was on her way down that yellow brick road, and nothing or no one could stop her. The day I saw that movie I was fascinated by those ruby red shoes as they begin to glow. I received my first pair of red shoes when my aunt went to see an oncologist. She wore her red shoes and walked in the doctor's office undefeated, and she wore them to every doctor's appointment after that. The scans of her liver showed spots on both of them. Although the answer my aunt received was not a good one, because cancer is never a good answer; she relied on her red shoes and the Universe for strength. My aunt walked through the next two years and six months fighting for her life. When you focus on the positive during a crisis with a pair of red shoes on, everything wrong will turn to right, that's what I believe. My red shoes are too good for school, but when I wear them on Valentine's Day I transform into a superhero that has the power to conquer the world, it's my way of being unstoppable.

Sometimes I don't know who I am when I put red shoes on. When I look in the mirror, I try to identify with that person I see. I know she is brown and beautiful with hues of colors; skin that's smooth without the reassurance of makeup. So many students at school wear eyeliner, eye shadow, foundation, and lipstick. I wonder what their parents say, or if they even know. Only clowns are supposed to wear makeup that's what mom said. I feel so special when I wear my red shoes. I smile a lot, I give a lot, and I help people feel special; at least I try by being kind to others.

There is a girl in my class who wore the same shoes for three straight years. They were a pair of brown soft sole Sketchers. I felt sorry for her as she was the "weird girl" in the class. I gave her lots of empathy and befriended her. Usually if the popular kids see you talking to a "weirdo" they think you're one too. I didn't want any labels and I don't care what they think of me either. I feel sorry for that girl because she doesn't have an opportunity to get new shoes, which is obvious. I get at least five pair of new shoes every year. I don't consider that a lot when some people spend thousands of dollars on one pair. Imagine what their closet looks like. The girl in my class will never experience the magic of shoes because she doesn't have enough. A teacher at school gives her a pair of old sneakers each year. One day the class went outside for PE and the girl walked in a pile of mud after Ms. Crystal announced that the grass was muddy. heard Ms. Crystal say, "do not step in the mud, you will ruin your sneakers". When it was time to come in the girl tracked mud all over the gym floor. Some kids just don't get it and that's why we need to help them. Instead, everyone laughed (including I) because the look on the girl's face, after the coach embarrassed her was too funny. The next day she came to school with a brand-new pair of white Skechers with a silver buckle on it, everyone was shocked. I gave her a compliment by saying "your shoes are nice", and she smiled all day. Then she gave a note from her mom for the teacher but showed me first. The note said, please keep my daughter out of mud she had to wear her church sneakers to school. I can't believe the girl is being deprived her of a shoe life, which is an opportunity to feel magical.

Popular boys are nothing without the magic of their shoes, on or off the court, and their shoe choice is often sneakers. I don't know why they love wearing that type of shoe, whatever the reason it works. Girls and women have more shoe options; boys and men have cool selections but limited selections for dressing up or down. I got it, the price for a pair of Jordan's automatically guarantees magic to happen. So that's why boys think they're popular. Oh yeah, celebrities love Jordan's too. Research shows that boys and men are smart, but girls and women are smarter. It's a theory of how the left and right side of the brain operates, which is different from female to male. Some girls worship the ground boys walk on, and fascinated by what they wear on their feet. A pair of sneakers gives the ego/ personality superpowers, and the will to conquer others. Sneakers are magical on the basketball court when the foot moves take on a different approach in every single game, some wins and some losses. The losing teams try their best to show their magic of their sneakers, and when there is no magic they become emotional. When men wear dress up shoes it makes them feel on top of the world. I asked Mr. popular, "How does he feel when wearing your favorite pair of sneakers on and off the court"? He said, "it feels like I control it all". Sneakers portray a hip-hop fashion look and most middle school boys want that image. To go through middle and high school without magic it's a hard and lonely life. Some students feel as if they are not good enough. I wonder if the geeks try to find shoe magic that will un-geek them. Geeks as we know are nerds, dweebs, jerks, and dorks are one of the same definition, basically smart but weird. Really, I think a geek is a smart person that uses their brain to think. Everyone has the potential to be a geek/smart.

Middle school is a challenge; everyone is expected to learn and pass state exams every year to move to prove your either smart or dumb. But not all students are smart enough to pass, some can only function on their cognitive level. The typical educational standards predict how well a student can receive, recall, and retain information. Mom said, more diverse school systems are needed to offer differentiated curriculums that provide a different set of standards. Testing students other than the paper and pencil method will help Students a passing grade based their level of achievement. I hear teachers debate all the time about the direction of education today. for all the hard work they do. They explain that education was a way to control certain groups of people therefore, people were denied an education, an opportunity to learn.

Things are different now but I always wonder why people were denied an education, an opportunity to reach their potential. Students that are labeled dumb have a hard time in school and throughout their lives. When my teacher asks, "who loves school", no one answered. Some students just think school is a chore that they should not have to do. Smart students love school but have social problems also get picked on, which can lead to self-esteem issues, problems making friends, and maintaining relationships with others. A personality disorder (a deeply ingrained and maladaptive pattern of behavior of a specified kind, typically manifest by the time one reaches adolescence. Causing long-term problems in relationships). What I don't understand is how the popular boys are really dumb, but they are most loved by their peers. They don't mind that having a bad boy reputation, going to alternative school, juvenile detention, or even jail. They don't care because they aren't smart enough too. In middle school, all boys and girls think about is who's popular and who's not. The smart boys have no girlfriends and the popular boys are the bullies that gets all the girls. Girls are bullies too so the same goes for them. that sounds backwards to me but that's how it goes. The purpose of a bully is to seek attention in front of a crowd. Groupies are kids that follow the bullies and their jobs are to recruit others to agree with bulling. Then they start bulling others just to win approval or seen as popular. Bullies do have shoe magic, but I'm not sure if they deserve it or not. Wearing magic shoes sends give a positive and loving vibration in the persons self-esteem. When low vibrations in the self is activated, the person as negative behavior responses.

I found out about the founders of the bullies' club in school. They are geeks that turned into bullies. So, I immediately went to my locker and put on my magic sneakers. I walked up to some of the groupies (girls) and said, "I know what you've done to Anaya and you will not get away with it this year". They looked at me and wondered where I came from since I'm new this year. I gave them a pamphlet on bullying then asked, "Why do you hurt others by harassing them"? One girl replied, "No reason". I said, "You should have a reason for everything you do in life, and if you don't have a reason for hurting unpopular girls then you need to stop". I asked if they have ever been bullied, one of the girls said "Yes. I asked how she felt by it, "not good" she said. But

I do it because it was done to me, and I'm just getting my payback". I asked the groupies to please stop hurting others, and to change their behaviors by posting positive messaging. I told one girl if she didn't like being bullied than no one else does either. My intentions was to tell the principal, but to my surprise they came to school the next day to protest. With picket signs that read, Stop The Bullying at School. They demonstrated their constitutional rights. The principals were unaware of the action taking place on school grounds in front of the building. Students have the right to express their freedom of speech, so they were allowed to protest until the bell rings. The principal called the local news media instead of getting upset, for a story that was aired on the nightly news. When I entered the school building, I looked at the girls and smiled. Then I looked down and noticed everyone wearing new shoes. The girls had on bright pink and the boy's wore baby blue. Wow, I thought shoe magic really works if you believe in the powers of the Universe.

If you wear the wrong shoes with the wrong outfit you will miss the magic of shoes. The right style and color of a shoe must compliment the outfit. If you wear shoes that is too old or worn no magic will occur. That's why That's why I will never buy used shoes again. I believe when you recycle shoes you might take on past drama. There is nothing to gain, no sparkles to see, and no magic of shoes. Everyone benefits from a color match just to see what truly compliments their skin tone. When and if there is a suggest match I say, stick to those colors in hues. My cousins in school studying to become a fashion stylist, and will began to be a fashion stylist, and will start a career at FIDM (Fashion Institute of Design & Merchandising) this year in LA (Los Angeles, California). Nia will create my prison through style, fashion, and color. She will also design the layout for my shoe. Store. Nia is lucky at eighteen to start a new life for herself away from home. Turning eighteenth is a big number, its freedom away from parents. Nia's worked her first job at a retail store, and on her eighteenth birthday, she got a new pair of shoes. Nia didn't believe she would get a job and that made her sad all the time. Her mother kept telling her to wait until she turns eighteen and see what happens. Nia didn't believe her. When Nia put on her new shoes for special day, she received a called with exciting news! Yes, congratulations your hired! She yelled; I believe in the magic of shoes!

The manager told Nia she prayed for her all night with her interview shoes still on until she heard from the store manager. The one thing that stood out about Nia was her friendly personality, her professional fashion attire, and shoes. Nia's has lots of shoes mainly sneakers, and loves dressing others including herself. She stays updated on fashion trends and knows all the stylish looks. Nia was popular in high school and the president of the fashion club. She has lots of followers and know what's hot and what's not for teens. When she was in LA visiting FIDM the school took students on a trip to the fashion district called Stantee Alley. Nia was in fashion heaven and said they have everything you can imagine. The street wear is a hip-hop look and always trending.

I asked Nia about the traditional look for boys and girls. For the boys, The collegiate look are strips and knit with cargo pants arc called comfy clothes. The Skater style is dark and baggy clothing with a t-shirt look and a pair of Timberland boots is a perfect match. The plaid look is Burberry or fake fur with Aldo boots, an awesome look for sure. For the girls, a rhinestone cowgirl style is western denim with boots, and a plaid shirt (eat your heart out Texas). But for the girl who likes to dress up, she wears a ruffle dress with a bow in the back. The athletic and casual look gives both boys and girls a choice in choosing their own style and sneakers are allowed. When it comes to fashion, either rich or poor young or old, fashion gives everyone a chance to dress up or down and the only one who really cares is you.

There is a community shoe dump in my town where citizens can get a used pair of shoes free of charge. The shoes look new and a second pair is only one dollar. This is a good service for families to meet their basic needs. More community leaders are needed to promote awareness and commit to service projects that involves and benefits everyone. The Universe is a place that provides and protects all living things only if we do our part. This place (Earth) we call home must be at peace and it's a collective effort. That's why community programs are needed to help families live a better life and get what they need. This type of community bonding helps students at home and school. I was talking to my teachers about kids that really need alternative educational learning programs to address all the social issues that teenagers are struggling with. Including their values, ethics, morals, abuse, low self-esteem, drugs, teen pregnancy, and the list goes on. Mom agrees that education in America must be reformed, and let parents get involved and vote on a differentiated curriculum. I like the idea of school uniforms because it creates unity. Having a standard look when going to school will eliminate a lot of negative talk and creates a climate to eliminate hostility between students. A goal of school reform can be as simple as helping students make better choices by practicing self-determination skills. All students can choose a pair of magic shoes, or sneakers by making an appointment for a shoe fitting at the beginning of the school year. During this appointment students can try on as many shoes as they like until they find the magical pair. They will know if the shoes are the right pair when the magic strikes. I have signs posted around the school telling kids about the magic of shoes, and everyone wants to know. I will not give away the secret because students must discover the magic on their own, but someone always ask me to be present at the appointment. I always say no. Then I thought about it, I can actually help the school environment by ensuring all students receive the right pair of shoes. OK, shoe magic will help students make positive decisions. The big secret is… magic shoes are the one and only pair (out of many) that will make someone feel different. A magical experience feels like an outer body encounter, something you can't explain. That's why I must be there to see what happens when the right shoes fit. There is more to the story, the magic of shoes is a gift of power that is given to help connect to someone's divine purpose. During a shoe fitting when I can't identify any magic, the student will need to reschedule. During the school year I see students that did not come back for another fitting. Because of that they are no magic of their shoes, and always in trouble.

Sometimes it's hard to choose the right pair of shoes for the day, Some people they just don't know how to style or mix match colors. If you pick out a random pair of shoes they might always remember; they might look appealing but are they magic? Be very careful about the shoes you choose. Why, may one ask? A person must try on several pairs first before knowing if, or if not, it matches your personality and outfit. All students must experience the magic of shoes why? It teaches self-determination skills and helps students gain awareness of themselves. My aunt in Texas is a teacher, so she teaches me a lot about character building and the art of giving and service. She sent me a big binder of information with worksheets and exercises to complete then practice the skill. I want to be the best version of me therefore, I will give myself balance, understanding, patience, and positive energy. I value myself; I am confident in who I am, and I working on a plan for my life to meet personal goals. I glanced through the chapters and thought, this is good information. Honesty is the best policy, mom said. Auntie Su teach online classes too, for her organization, she said if students are never taught they will never learn. It's hard to teach adults what they didn't learn as a child.

Self-Determination is:

- Making Choices
- Decision Making
- Problem-Solving
- Independent Living Skills
- Risk Taking
- Safety
- Goal Setting
- Attainment
- Self-Observation
- Evaluation
- Reinforcement
- Self-Instruction
- Self-Understanding
- Self-Advocacy
- Leadership
- Positive self-esteem
- Outcome Expectancy
- Internal Locus of Control

The classes I'm taking with auntie are teaching me how to practice the skills of self-determination. In the process of life there is a structure, a class, a lesson to learn, and a book to read; to learn the art of life. Learning how to practice the skills through real life scenarios helps me to understand myself, my personality, and what I stand for. As a committee member, I pitched an idea of a school-wide campaign to offer weekend classes. This will give all students an opportunity to understand themselves through the self-determination goals. With so many behavior issues in school, creating a program for troubled students will help them acknowledge themselves and their actions. I know that if I refused to seek help when I'm in trouble, I risk losing everything. At home I have reinforcements from mom and the elders in my family. One of my tools to redirect negativity is defined as a writing activity, and a daily goal to model. After learning each goal students are monitored and track their own progress. My aunt offers a parenting class and professional development credits after taking the course. Humans must acknowledge our responsibility to the Universe, and prove we are better than what statistics say we are. Statistics also show, children can grasp logic and conceptual learning in early stages of development.

Children around the world still do not have access to basic needs. Including walking the streets and dirt roads without shoes on. Students shamed one another at school for what they don't have. In today's society footwear is a sign of civilization, but in America if you walk outside barefoot, it's a sign of mental disorder/illness. I look at bare feet as a sign of cultural differences and a natural state of being. It's against the law in civil societies to enter a public place barefooted. I don't know if my family is considered above or below the poverty line, but I like walking barefoot. I also see celebrities walking around barefooted too, which shows unity. Footwear does provide protection from cuts, abrasions, bruises, objects on the ground. How about frostbites and parasites, so that's a reason for me to wear shoes outside. There is shoe magic in bare feet, but it's another level of understanding. I'll miss all the rewards that are due to me if I don't wear shoes. I don't like the texture of the Terrain (only grass) on my bare feet outside. Some shoes can limit the flexibility and mobility of the foot, which leads to accidents. Bare feet have a natural gait to allow a rocking motion. In current society, footwear is used for fashion and social norms.

I sent a pair of shoes to my dad's village for a holiday gift to a random person, practicing the goal of giving. I told dad to give the shoes to someone that really, really needs them. I brought a pair for a teenager or young adult. Dad followed through with my wish of a random act of kindness. He used a method that allowed the gift to be given to the perfect person, and he didn't tell me his shoe secret. When dad called, he told me a young man received the gift. I was so happy! That guy had only one pair of old Shoes. He prayed for a new pair before starting a new job in the city. He didn't want to look as if he walked from the village. He also wanted to look well-groomed with new clothes and shoes. He worried for a month about how he would look for his first job. The The young man prayed every day and every hour, then dad knocked on his door and said, "hello I have a gift for you". His eyes lit up, and dad saw glowing stars in his eyes When the young man put on his shoes, he started Jumping. He continued jumping for hours. Everyone in the village gathered around him and started jumping to, but didn't know why. They knew he was celebrating his new shoes. But after hours of jumping, a local doctor realized something was wrong. Several people tried to stop him by holding him still then laying him on the ground. He was so exhausted and passed out. After waking up the next morning, he wondered what happened to him. Dad carried the man home and put him in bed. Then took off the new shoes and back in box. The man thought it was all a dream when he woke up until he saw the shoe box. He started smiling then opened the box again to confirm his prayers was answered.

The new job will start in two days, so he put all his clothes together for the week and matched them with his one pair of shoes. Dad asked him to throw away the old shoes. Before the young man complied, he wore the old shoes to visit the chief of his village. He asked the chief to gather the village community so he can make an announcement. "Energy is Alive", and it has prevailed through me and touched my chakras that activated the spirits. Everyone wished him well as he moved away from the village for the very first time. He will honor his tradition and duty of sharing his money with the village. Then he walked around with a smile all day, and couldn't sleep that night. The thoughts of a new life were overwhelming. The next morning, the man put on his new shoes and started jumping before stepping outside. After five minutes of jumping, he sat down then realized those shoes from America are magical. He was able to calm himself down by deep breathing to get to work on time. The young man spent the rest of his life working, saving money, being happy, and grateful to buy more shoes.

I'm going to the eighth-grade prom this year, I've been looking forward to this since six-grade. Although this is not an official date, I'm meeting up with friends then hang out with a boy who ask me the be his date at the prom. I first have to ask mom can go since I'm only in the seventh grade. Knowing mom it's a yes so, I told Malik to call me later. Yes, we talked later about what to wear and color coordination. Malik is from South Africa that's what I heard anyway, and he confirmed it. I asked, what's his favorite color, and he mentioned that he loves to dress up in color combinations. I have a cousin named Malik so that's a bonus for him. He's tall, slim, good looking, muscles, nice hair, and very dark skinned! I'm not into boys like that, but some are cool to talk to. Mom asked, "does he have his head on his shoulders. When speaking to Malik, his voice sounds different on the phone, like he's giving a speech with an accent, "Hello this is Malik may I speak to Sheba please". I guess he thought it was my mother, "Yes, this is Sheba", and the conversation continued from there. We talked about the prom, what time to meet up, and where. I told him I will be with other groups of friends that include boys, he is free to hang out with other girls too. Because everyone has choices, and we are only friends. We agreed on a color scheme, his favorite color is orange. Of course, my color hues of green and pink will not work them together. So, there's a color issue and it's beyond black and white.

I will use my color vision to create a new color hue of two or more colors. Green and orange with a mixture of white gives a light brownish orange type color, but if I add more orange to the brownish color. The color leans more toward an orange. If I use less orange, I will have more of a greenish color, and pink is out of the equation. Either way

I don't like the color, but it must work. I will use accessories and find shoes that pop (compliment the dress). I told Malik we should shop together to come up with nice prom attire. I looked online for shoes, although I can consider looking in my closet, looking for a matching hue of the color maybe challenging. A fabric store could be the next option. If we don't find the, a color change to the orange family will do. Mom thought it would be a good idea to make my dress, which will be the only way to get the color I want. I think we should look slightly different from one other, so it doesn't appear we're dating. Malik's idea is to wear African attire, and that's when I said "oh yeah that's right, you are from South Africa". I told him all about my dad, which he knew from the summer trip to Africa. Malik said he wanted to go on the trip but couldn't, so he heard all about it, of course he did.

The idea of African attire at a prom doesn't sound good to me. It means we are dating, and I don't want to give that impression. On Saturday mom took us to the mall first and then to the fabric store. I asked Malik to wear his favorite shoes, and I will do the same. He didn't ask way. We went to every clothing store for formal/semi-formal wear and couldn't find anything. So, we are headed to the fabric story. I had a color swatch, and went straight to the salesclerk for help. We were out of the store in twenty minutes because we found the perfect fabric. Mom finished my dress a week before the prom. When I tried it on with my shoes I turned into a Princess. Malik just rented a tux and mom made his shirt out of an orange hue. We look fabulous together and no one will ever know that I think Malik is #number1. With the perfect pair of shoes, I don't want our shoe color to match for obvious reasons. They won't because he will wear a basic black shoe. Malik's shoes are new, he brought them at the mall; I found a pair online. Kids are talking about wearing the hottest pumps and looking their absolute best. Why not, it's the prom. Turn Up! This is the occasion for formal wear.

Today is the day everyone's been waiting for, it's the Prom. Some students arrive in limousines and luxury cars, they walked, and some are dropped off by parents. Others are late because they couldn't get a ride, but whatever it took to get there everyone showed up. We are having the best time ever! The Prom is turned up, and the girls are wearing shoes they could hardly walk in. If you're going to wear high heels you should certainly practice first. I will only wear heels if they support my feet, and comfortable for dancing. I arrive by parent drop off; Malik was there hanging out with friends. I walked up to him just as he turned around and said, "You look gorgeous". I smiled so hard my cheeks are hurting trying not to be so obvious that I like him. We headed to the dance floor and everyone is looking at us (in my head); I'm a little nervous. I immediately separate myself from Malik after we danced by getting in line for snacks.

The night is early, and people are still arriving to the prom late. Malik and I took pictures with a few people in line. Then I see heads turning looking at us, we must look good together. At this point everyone assumed we came together, and I didn't try to defend myself. I just let people think whatever they want. We decided to hang out for the rest of the night and had a really good time together. Boyfriend! If mom heard that word, she would Ask for the meaning of the compound word, Boyfriend. I'm not allowed to date boys until I am 21, that's a family rule. Mom said, I will be able to make mature decisions by then. We danced again and I heard my name then Malik's called to the stage. We were voted best dress; I received a bouquet of roses and Malik was given a corsage. We took more pictures for the yearbook receiving our plaque, and both of us feeling like celebrities. Now that I think about it, I actually created my own fifteen minutes of fame.

Mom picked me up, and I offered Malik a ride home and he accepted. His family invited us in for cup of tea. As the adults talked about Africa, Malik and I talked about starting high school next year. I told him I don't mind a friendship but not a girlfriend. I will not date until college, my rules (and mom's) based on so many things. My friends don't understand rules that's why they need self-determination goals. I am protecting myself, my heart, and feelings from getting broken for reasons I will not understand. Mom wants us to focus on education and work towards a career first. Mom said, "boys can really destroy the future of a young girl if her head is not on her Shoulders". If you don't believe in yourself, you can easily be influence by others. Mom doesn't hide the truth about her past relationships with former male friends and husbands. She talks about her stories so we can learn from her mistakes. I agree with mom's philosophy and expectations of her daughters, it represent excellence. All I know and will continue to do, is listen to my parents and elders that share their stories about what this life is about.

Shoe Secrets

I am not old enough to have a job, so I babysit for money. At eight years old I thought about dollars and cents, sold greeting cards, made Barbie doll clothes, and sold them to family and friends. Money management is a skill worth learning, so learned about budgets to manage my spending habits. Money skills help prepare me for a popup shoe sale. My mother is not a millionaire according to the US Government class status, so my sister and I receive shoes only when we need them. Occasionally, we get new shoes from family members for birthdays or Kwanzaa gifts. Every time I ask mom for shoe money she explains why, "I can't afford to buy another pair of shoes, every time you want new shoes so does *La-La,* that's two pairs at once". So, I would deliberately damage my shoes just to get a new pair Then, *La-La* would have to wait a long time for her new shoes. That's not right; it's deceiving and against my values, so I'm feeling bad about my decision. I must redeem myself one day but for now, *La-La* will never know this shoe secret. She does wonder and question why I always have a problem with my shoes, LOL. I had to do whatever, by any means necessary to get what I want, a new pair of shoes. I'm sorry, it's a shoe obsession!

My shoe secrets are about indulging in what drives my passion, so I spend time online browsing through shoe sites. Also, reading about who wears what on their feet (celebrity) and bookmarking all the shoe sales; getting ready to spend. I browse all the global websites and all types of shoes for entertainment. If I had money, I would pop into a shoe shopping spree; spending whatever for the cost to buy whatever I want. Since I am also fascinated about printing or cutting out pictures of shoes from online images and magazines. I created a shoe catalog that has over six thousand pairs of paper shoes. I've been collecting pictures from magazines for over five years.

Every time I visit grandma the first thing I do is go straight to her shoe closet and just sit on the floor to enjoy the smell of her new shoes. The smell of leather is very distinctive and drives my senses wild. Being around so many shoes, helps me to envision my closet store. I like to play shoe games by lining up shoes according to the occasion, color, and type. Then I label the categories by brands, this creates an access for customers to grab and go. My footwear categories are sneakers, flip flops, loafers, crocks, leather sandals, pumps, stilettos, dress up, boots, water shoes, and yes slippers. I prefer wearing flat shoes and only pumps when appropriate with a dress or skirt. Yes pumps are girly, and since I am a girl I have to wear them occasionally. Sneakers, in my opinion, are only for the gym, exercising, playing ball or walking in the park. The dress code at school is sneakers Everyday. I like when students wear other footwear options to express themselves. My cousin in Texas (Nia) wears only sneakers and her collection combined with her sister's (Asa) is huge! Just like the boys, girls wear sneakers too. I will not wear just sneakers, although they are the most comfortable for your feet. Flip flops are the absolute worst! They damage the feet and they have no structure. I analyze everything including shoes that make senses and ones that don't. I will welcome a pair of flip flops in my closet only when I am taking a shower in a foreign.

My love for sandals comes from a traditional and family practice that built my desire for shoes. I always think of my African ancestors in the diaspora and how they have endured the impossible; like walking for miles barefoot. Mom bronzed our first pair of baby shoes to remember the story of the Stone Age, and the Paleolithic times (prehistoric before humans). The importance of what proper footwear meant to those who received sandals for the very first time. I treasure leather sandals and what they stand for. I felt bad about dad's tradition of shoes, not having baby shoes. The agony of suffering and not able to protect his feet, that worried me for a long time. My goal is to work hard in life to help those in need of shoes, and travel the globe to give people a proper shoe fitting to walk in comfort. In America we have the luxury of getting to and from places before walking. There are trains, planes, automobiles, buses, bikes, boats, skates, scooters, and we only walk when we want to, not because we have too. My collection of sandals is limited to eight pairs, the cheap ones keep breaking and the leather ones I preserve. I will not wear sandals if I can't smell the leather. I treat my sandals like gold, watching were I step, who I stepped to, and no water allowed. When it rains it pours and I enjoy walking in the rain with my bare feet.

I consider pumps the dress up shoe that's worn with formal attire. For example, weddings, award dinners, graduation and any dress that requires a dressy dress. I like dress up shoes but I will only wear them when necessary because they are very uncomfortable for me. Celebrities walk with grace, I know they have foot pain at some point, but everyone wants to follow their shoe path anyway. In the early days of shoe fashion, heels were no higher than an inch and now present day, heels can be as high as the ceiling. I remember playing dress up with mom's high heels. I would walk around the house trying not to fall, but when I did *La-La* laughed so hard she made me cry. It was not so funny when I fell down the steps and could have broken bones. Then *La-La* broke a pair of mom's heels she tried on, and mom was FURIOUS! Casual shoes are the best, I wear them when I dress up and down. It's the shoe with the most variety.

The best shoe category for me are boots for the winter. Technically, boots can be worn all year and useful in cold weather, boots keep me warm too. I love all boot styles especially riding boots. Boots are too hot for summer temperatures, let's not forget they were created for the cold weather only. I personally think it's a fashion mistake to wear boots when it's 110 degrees outside, but remember fashion has no rules anymore. I had an idea one day to dye my boots, my color of choice. I took tan boots and dyed them teal. I discovered the color teal from Nia, her mom painted her room teal with a desk against the wall to match. Teal was a hard color to find in a dye. During the process, I couldn't get the perfect color, who would really dye boots besides me, so I ruin my boots. I knew I was in big trouble if mom found out. I had to get rid of the boots some kind of way and without anyone knowing. This time it will not be so easy because the boots are new. I don't know what to do, so I throw them away in a dumpster. I told no one about the accident including *La-La,* I knew she would tell mom for sure. When mom asked me, "where are the boots" I lied! Telling her I accidently left them over auntie's house. She gave me a hard stare and said, "the next time you go over there, get them". I pretended to look for my boots the next day at auntie's house, but just couldn't find them I told mom. I was scared and that's why I lied, but mom knew I was not telling the truth. Although I thought I got away with it, mom promised that she will never buy me another pair of boots for the rest of my life.

Shoe secrets do have consequences when you try to hide the truth. My friends say that slippers do not have a place in fashion because they are not shoes. I agree but as yes they are as long as they have a sole it's considered footwear. I tried to explain the history of shoes to my friends; they don't want to hear about it. Slippers have the same standards of covering the feet just like any other sole. They were designed from felt and worn by many factory workers to keep their feet warm, and comfortable on cold stone floors in the 1800s. Warmth and comfort goes with slippers, and every home should have at least one pair. The sales of slippers made big numbers in sales, and that's how they became famous.

After the second shoe project and summer trip, I became known for helping others. I earned the respect from my peers and became Miss Popular. I raised the conscious level for many students and changed their belief system that strengthen their self-worth. I wanted the bullies to unite and stop hurting people, I accomplished that. At the end of the school year all the campuses in thethe campuses in district hosted an awards ceremony; for academic excellence and community achievement. The student council members were invited from each school and given a table to represent their campus. Each school was encouraged to show school spirit, and present a visual presentation of a goal accomplished for the year. A winner will be announced at the end of the ceremony. My school presented a shoe theme, and the opening page was a big red shoe highlighted in rhinestones. I introduced our school theme to the audience; The Magic of Shoes - A journey through middle school with the right pair of shoes on. My team members are dressed in red shoes with matching white dresses, so we needed to feel the magic from our shoes. all feel and receive shoe magic that night. The ceremony started and the atmosphere was glowing with excitement. If my school receives recognition tonight for meeting the criteria, our team will become educational celebrities. Next was a formal dinner leading up to guest speakers then the award ceremony. We heard the announcement… and the winner is. At that moment I took a deep breath, then I heard our schools called. Everyone gasped for air with their hands on their mouth, we all exhaled when the speaker called our team to the stage. The award was a plaque for outstanding community service. What a magical event!

I thought about having a theme party at my house inviting the elite group of students from school; just because it's a good social activity. I will invite all the bullies and tell them to wear a fresh pair of shoes that matches my theme color fuchsia. I can't wait to see how many people will come up that I invite. I got excited about the possibilities of the party. I will make invitations in a fuchsia card stock with black lettering and gold circles that reads: VIP Party FYI ONLY Save The Date… I personally gave invitations to the first fifty people labeled bullies. They were hesitant to take the envelope I gave them. When I passed by the VIP crowd after school, they all looked at me with a nod confirming their attendance. I asked mom if I can have a party hoping she will say yes, and she did! So now I have a week to plan it. I confirmed with my aunt about hosting the party at her house before giving out the invitations. My aunt's house will accommodate all fifty bullies if they show up, I think they will. My aunt loved the concept of a party and how I'm inviting students that need the most attention. This is a way to improve their self-esteem. My uncle is a police officer, so I asked him to chaperone the party and he won't be in uniform. I don't want any fights to happen at my aunt's house. I wanted my uncle to look more like a bouncer dressed in black. A bouncer is another word for security guard. Invitations only are required to get in this party. I wrote on the invention in big bold letters, INVITATION IN HAND TO GET IN! I (the host) will be standing at the door with security to make sure everything's good.

It's party time, I love a good party and ready to get the party started! I hung up a few decorations including a disco ball and LED lights. I also hired a real DJ (AsaAce). The bouncer will give each individual or group a few party rules and pep talk for acknowledgement and compliance. He will also do a pat down for any contraband or weapons. The party's starting with a few VIPs arriving. I start to feel strange, like having an outer body experience. A little scared and nervous, never done this before. I greet everyone with welcomes and lead time in the party. In doors and out for fresh air as needed is available. I want everyone to feel comfortable and safe. It's amazing to see everyone all fuchsia out, now that is unity. The styles are up to part, meaning they could certainly make the red carpet. My uncle said we should stream the party, "OK that sounds great", I said. He knows what going on with the VIPs at school, I told him. This party is so important it should be streamed on all platforms. The VIPs are making a difference by agreeing to stop the hate. They are committed to learning self-determination skills to think, and respond to peers differently. This party allow them VIPs to let their guard down and acknowledge who they are and what they done. OK America let's take bullying to another level by using emotional intelligence to stop hurting others. Most VIPs want to change their behavior of being mean to others, only if they knew how. I want this party to have a great impact on the population, and culture in public school systems in America and globally. Being a teenager is complicated but after COVID-19 it become difficult to handle emotionally. Aggressive student behavior comes from a pattern of childhood wounds, that forms self-esteem issues in the formative years. Bullies were bullied too the cycle continued, and they will be stopped. All negative energy need is love; love is positive energy. Everyone's shoes look magical, so I'm predicting a victory. This party is a BIG deal and a secret. don't want any social media exposure yet, so I told my uncle no streaming. The AsaAce is playing all the radio music, and everyone is hyped. My goal is to get everyone to mingle. The party starts at 9:00pm and twenty people was at the door already. By 9:30pm all fifty guest was counted for. A few uninvited guests from the neighborhood, but we were prepared for intruders. The regular students wanted to be bullies just to come to the party, only if they knew about it. With a blow of confetti, the party officially started at 9:31pm.

Doors shut! No more arrivals expected, and we are ready for take-off. The house party is on lock down, my uncle will secure the perimeter.. My aunt made a party schedule, apparently she has a secret agenda for this party, so all I had to do was act like a celebrity. I made sure I welcomed everyone by being up close and personal. Even though I gave everyone an invitation I don't know them personally, This is a chance to learn who's who quick. With a clip board in my hand, I shook hands and ask for names, numbers, email addresses, and social media links., With a brief conversation and a quick rapport, I thanked everyone for showing up and took a group picture together. I mentioned my concern about keeping this party confidential as they all agreed. My aunt had something planned every thirty minutes to keep the party going. This party is a hit and, it's going down for real! Good music and good energy as everyone is dancing and have a good time. This party was the right thing to do. With no disorderly conduct, it's amazing how a group of bad kids are not so bad after all. There is good in everyone. Everyone escaped into the night air looking up at the sky full of stars. We danced, ate, played games, and I gave out prizes before my uncle announced a VIP guest at the door. A secret guest I knew nothing about, then the music stops! My uncle shouts, "Let's welcome TI Atlanta's own celebrity is in the house". The crowd goes wild as he walks in the door and the noise level was extremely high. He performed one song, took pictures with everyone and gave a speech on bulling others. He wants us to start an anti-bulling campaign that he will sponsor.

Highlight of the party. He signed sneakers, shirts, bare skin, and whatever was available for a temporary tattoo of his signature. The What a great experience and the party ended with a BANG, and we gave the VIP an additional thirty minutes to process their thoughts of the party before leaving. OMG… the party is over. I stayed the night to help clean up. I can't wait for school on Monday to see the behaviors of the VIPs, and if they said anything about the party. At the end of the day, I heard no whispers about the party. I've been getting smiles and nods all day from the VIPs. It's not safe yet… I know the secret party will get out soon, I'm just waiting. After two weeks not a word circulating about the party. The VIPs pretended as if they don't know me when others are around, what a good idea I thought. As soon as

I see a VIP alone in the hall, they Whisper to me, "when is the next secret event?". I think it's safe to believe bullies have heart and They stick together in harmony.

I'm planning another exclusive VIP party because they asked and kept their promise to stay silent. I never heard a word. Wow! I respect them now and embrace the change they made as a group. Teamwork makes the dream work, that's what mom said. So, another theme party and another rapper, I will do my best. I'll talk to my uncle but the stakes will be higher this time. Meaning that it will cost MONEY, and the rapper may want a video stream live during the party. I don't know, it's still a risk for exposure for the VIPs to be seen in public. I held a meeting to discuss an organizational strategy for the party. We talked through the intervention plan for next party, and TI's anti-bulling campaign. The VIPs wanted to reach out to other school district bullies and get them involved. The mission of the campaign is for each person to give back to others. By providing a safe space for the people they hurt the most. The event (instead of party) will take place at school. We agreed to start a VIP party club that includes a monthly donation. All current members joined by signing an agreement to acknowledge the conditions of participation. It's amazing to be a part of a secret club at school. I told the club (VIPs) members about having a Valentine's Day party. Everyone agreed on the idea and asked if they can secretly set it up. "No problem, let's make it happen", I said. The first thing to do is get approval from the principal, and present the idea to the student council about sponsoring theme parties throughout the school year. This is an opportunity for student council to raise money and promote social emotional learning. The tickets will cost $5.00 for all students.

The VIPs are organized and asked questions about the action plan for the party. With the school board's approval, the VIPs started marketing the party to student council members, parents, and every student in school. I look for good news stories when watching TV, so I found a headline story that read, Bullies Are Heroes After All. I wonder why the media always show the negative and the worst in people. My job for the event is to oversee the VIPs. They willsetup, decorate, provide snacks, make a playlist for DJ AsaAce. I told the council members to recruit students for voluntteering at the party, so we can be present and oversee everything. It's party time! When the doors opened the entire student body was waiting. To my surprise everyone is wearing red shoes with white tops. At that moment I cried, I felt the magic of shoes and I knew the night was going to be special. The décor was red pink and white with hearts all over the gym. Love is in the air tonight. I don't know who organized the footwear, I guess the VIPs, but it looks amazing. Prizes will be given for the best dress, the best shoes, and the best school spirit. When the special guest arrived, the VIPs stopped the music and made an announcement. "Our special is here yall, come on in, the one and only Chris Brown is in the house". He heard about the dance and wanted to support the champaign. Everyone lost their mind by screaming as loud as they could.

Now everybody wants to be my BFF's (best friend forever). So, now I'm real busy on the weekends with shopping, movies, games, dancing with entertaining friends. During the week I study do homework and take online classes. Mom does not let us just sit around idle; by watch TV, on our phones, or hanging out with friends. I know mom sounds strict, but she keeps us focused on the future. I take dance class twice a week and options to participate in school sports. Mom also teaches the practice of meditation and al the universal components of it. Such as grounding, crystals, chakras, and sound healing. Family is important, so my cousin (Naeesa) teaches us our African culture once a month. I look forward to family visits. She takes us shopping for shoes, which mom disapproves of at times. I aways came back with at least one pair, and would merge them into the closet with the other shoes. Mom will never know! On the weekends I can hang out with friends at the mall. Mom drops me off and picks me up, we normally start off with a movie and agree on what to watch, then window shop for shoes. Mom told me not to go in stores if I'm not spending money, and that's another rule. It makes sense to me, why torture myself when I can't buy shoes. What mom doesn't know is that I always have money for shoes. Mom window shops too when there's a shoe sale. I told Naeesa I want for a new pair of sandals for the summer, but mom insists I have enough after she surveyed my closet.

I heard screaming from someone in the mall, so I walked to the stores to see what's happening. I was shocked to see Naeesa's friend in handcuffs. I see merchandise in the police officer's hand that looks like a pair of sandals. What was that girl thinking of stealing a pair of sandals, people were whispering. I am so glad that I was not in the store with her, or nowhere near because I could have been labeled a thief. That would have ruined my reputation in school, and I probably would have been kicked out of the mall forever! I don't know that girl and hope this news doesn't circulate. To my surprise the girl was released and given a ticket, but she had to appear in court. I didn't hear a word about it in school, and wasn't going to say anything either. Naeesa said the girl was stealing those sandals for me. She's a senior at school, when I ran into her on Monday I gave her the biggest hug and apologized, for the incident. I didn't want her to know that I knew she stole for me. Secrets are told every day by the young and old, the short and tall, by husbands and wives, girlfriends and boyfriends, and yes teachers and students. They tell tall tales (a lie) instead of the truth, but why?

The compounds that make up materials of a shoe will break down causing your shoes to fall apart over time. Just like other rubber products on the market; tires, gloves, rubber bands, seal rings, shoe soles, and let's not forget about the rubber duckies. Rubber only last for a limited time before the composition of materials break down. For a quick science lesson, the word vulcanization is a chemical process for converting natural rubber into more durable materials. When adding sulfur or other equivalent materials to the mix, that's the short version. Leather is more durable and more expensive, but it maintains a longer shelf life than rubber. I thought I could keep my shoes forever, but according to the shoe experts they should be replaced every three to five hundred miles. It's possible that shoes can age if they just sit around and never walk. So how do I get to know them, by wearing them to school one day. After wearing the old shoes that sat in my closet for years they fell apart. I loved those shoes the moment I laid eyes on them. After two hours of walking up and down the halls the rubber sole on my left shoe completely came off before getting to class. I never expected any shoe to fail while walking, but it did. I had no spear shoes that day so walked barefoot, how embarrassing. I remember a camping trip one summer, it was one of the hottest summers on record. With a heat index of 115 degrees, this camping trip ruined my sandals by the raves of the sun melting them. Heat and rubber creates a compound reaction that is not environmentally friendly.

The real desert heat is when my family and I went to visit relatives in Sudan, Central Africa. Mom traced her family heritage to the Sudan North Africa, so we planned a trip to Africa for a visit. Our relatives have been searching for us, their American family for centuries. I wasn't interested in going because of the heat, and what will happen to my sandals. Also the safety issues as the country is at war through ethnic cleansing or genocide. Mom said we have to go because an elder family member spent her life looking for family members that was taken from their village. Mom was told a living elder has passed down the family story of stolen family members from their village. Her great, great, great, great grandmother witnessed two brothers being hand cuffed with rope and taken to the sea. They board a big ship, was called human cargo, and was a part of the Trans-Atlantic Slave Trade. As a child she never forgotten family stories that was told to keep their African culture alive. The relatives sponsored the trip and took care of all the expenses during our visit. It's hard to be in another African country and see more suffering. It breaks my heart and weights on my soul. I have to go mom said, and there is nothing she can do about the way I feel but she understands. I took two pairs of sandals and two pairs of sneakers, which are shoes from the I donation box. The red dirt will mess up a pair of good shoes. So, I did something against my shoe rules: I brought pleather sandals. The life span of this type of sandal is short lived. I agreed to wear them for this trip only then trash them before I leave. My sandal collection has traveled many miles because they are dependable. I normally travel with my favorite Sandals, it's my favorite type of shoe! From New York to St. Louis, Chicago back to St. Louis then to Atlanta, and Virginia Beach to Dallas/Fort Worth my sandals never failed me. Because I substituted leather sandals for fake ones I was humiliated when the strap broke. I'll walk carefully in my second pair that I will wear for the next four days. I have other things to worry about other than shoes breaking down when I need to focus on the purpose of this visit at this moment.

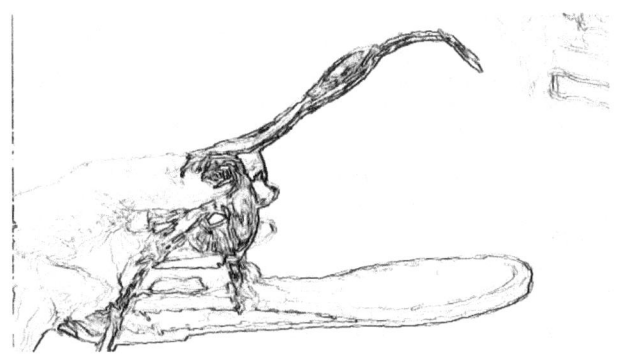

Another day here in Africa as we start the morning with family, prayer, and blessings. We are dressed in our African attire, which is traditional dressing to meet the relatives. I'm so glad I have the white sandals as they will match any print, traditional or not; it's a neutral tone. Reminiscing on all the pass memories of wearing my favorite sandals, I feel proud. My nostalgic (sentimental) memories of sandals are buying them on the first day of summer, and putting them on my feet. What a feeling… I'll be starting this summer in a strange place without a new pair of leather sandals. I always try to share peace, joy, and happiness to others by giving advice to life's issues. Right now I need to fell joy within myself by letting nothing, or no more destroy my inner peace. Knowing that I'm in Africa again I feel different and my spirit feels right. It's a feeling I can't quite explain, but I feel like I belong here. As I thought more about what was guiding my state if It's the connection to my culture, my tradition, and my freedom. It was not the magic of my shoes for this feeling, but accepting who I am and my culture that I carry within me.

Waking up in Africa feels amazing yet different. I'm thinking about red clay dirt. Wearing the same fake sandals for weeks is scary, I don't trust them. It's hard to let go of a favorite pair of shoes especially when I am forced to put certain shoes in retirement, ordered by mom. Old shoes should not be worn, it's too risky. I don't know why I want to hang on to them. I guess I want the world to know that they are not dead yet even when the sole falls off. Today breakfast consist of; fruit salad, English shortbread cookies, tea, water, and coffee. We are ready to go as the car arrives. We will meet mom's ancestors and the eldest living relative and the chief of the village. When the car pulls up everyone gets in. We are off to see the family down a very rocky road. Upon our arrival to the village I'm feeling nervous as I reach for my extra shoes before getting out of the car. It's not there, I left them in the lobby! OMG! The driver called the hotel to ask about a blue bag in a chair. Yes, they have it and will hold it at the front desk for me. I'm exhaling... what a relief. So, I slowly get out of the car hoping nothing goes wrong with the fake sandals. The minute I put my right foot on the ground I slipped and almost fell. I refuse look down. I pretend this is not happening again. The right sandal feels loose but I keep on walking a short distance to the circle of family.

Wow! I see a strong resemblance of my mother then I was convinced this is my family. Everyone gave us hugs and greet us with gifts and food. Then mom was given a special gift but will open it later. The celebration started with dancing then lunch. I danced to the rhythm of drums and I felt my right foot rubbing against the ground. Then I finally looked down and the left sandal was dangling by shreds, and the right was completely gone, LOL. I laughed so hard that everyone nearby laughed with me as they pointed at my feet. A relative about my age said something in his language that I didn't understand, then he point at my feet. Another relative said something to mom and gave me a pair of flip flops. I wasn't sure about putting them on and wanted to say no thank you, but that would be considered rude. In African culture, you bring gifts when visiting and you accept gifts that are given to you. I wanted to walk barefoot like my African family, it's a practice of grounding with earth elements and a part of the tradition.

The elder member came out to greet mom. Everyone in the village gathered around waiting for the elder to speak, which was interpreted for us. She motioned for mom to come closer to her then grabbed her hands and begin speaking. In summary of her statement, she is the last living relative at one hundred twenty years old (hard to believe I thought) and tells the family story that was pass down for generations. A family member witnessed the capture of three men from their village, one of the men belonged to their family. She explained, there were strange men that looked like ghosts. Members from the village fought with men that worked for the ghost to release the captured men. She waited all her life to hear news about her stolen family member but she never did. Her prayers were answered now that mom was found she is so happy and can now rest in peace. Her health is declining fast, and she is ready to meet her ancestors in the spiritual realm. The elder asked mom about her gift. The driver brought the box from the car. Mom finally opened the gift box and pulled out a stack of Africa money. The elder said, "This is for you and your family". Everyone cried as they were full of emotions. Mom said no she couldn't take the money. I whispered to mom that she had too, it would be an insult if she didn't. Mom promised to give the money to the village that needs an intergraded water system, a sustainable electric power source, infrastructure of roads, an upgraded school, and general resources for a better quality of life in the village. "I am a part of this village as this is my home too", mom said. Before leaving the village everyone gathered in prayer. Then I was handed another gift from someone who noticed what happened to my sandal. To my surprise it was a new pair of leather sandals, the smell of leather was absorb through my nostrils. A sense of calming overcame me and I couldn't stop smiling.

One last visit to the village to say farewell before heading to the airport. When we arrived, the family informed us that the elder transitioned after our visit with her. I cried as talked to the relatives about her life. No one in knew she was saving all that money hoping her family would return to Africa. I wore my new sandals traveling back home, and they are comfortable! My level of happiness increases when I get a new pair of shoes, but the African sandals feel different. The energy I have with these sandals on is special. The mission for mom is to take care of her village as promised to her ancestor. I felt positive energy on the journey overseas back home to America. I placed my new sandals safely on the shelf in my closet.

A Walk in My Shoes

Everyone, young, old, rich, poor, strong, and weak complains about their feet hurting. So, why do we experience foot pain when shoes are made for comfort. I will never pay hundreds or thousands of dollars for a single pair of shoes, rich or not. There are so many people in the world that does not have access to a decent pair of shoes. This creates long term foot problems. A good pair of shoes strengthen the sole of the foot. It's selfish to spend a large amount of money on one pair of footwear, celebrity or not. I asked mom about how a select group of people become celebrities. I think all people should have celebrity status due to their human rights. I want to know how I can become a celebrity even though I am one, but I need to make the money they do. If I can get my celebrity status, I will have lots of money to buy all the shoes in the world or at least some from every continent. With my average family budget I am limited on what I can buy but with my human rights, I will make Headline news for awareness of how we can save the planet Earth. How to prevent hunger, and how to have inner peace. After researching the definition of a celebrity - also referred to as a celeb in pop culture, is a person who has a prominent profile and commands a great degree of public fascination and influence. Then I asked myself, fascination – the capability of eliciting intense interest, being very attractive to someone or something, the state of being. So, what's the word eliciting to bring or draw out something dormant or hidden.

My dad walked miles with no shoes on. I remember walking to school with a hole in my shoes. It was nothing I could do but wait until mom was able to buy me a new pair. Dad on the other hand was accustom to walking with no shoes, saving his one good pair for church. Single parents try really hard to manage the responsibilities of raising a family alone. I wonder about mom's wellbeing and health, it's not easy but mom does a great job providing for us. La La and I will always respect our mother. Mom teaches us values, morals, and ethics to live our best life and get along with others at school and in communities. Wearing puniforms in elementary school made it easier to blend black or blue shoes that was required. Now in middle school I wear regular clothes, my wardrobe stresses me out because I need more clothes and shoes. I get frustrated competing with other girls over fashion. Sometimes I cry but not letting anyone, hear or see my tears. I wish my life was different, I wish I had more clothes for my shoes. There are so many things in life I don't understand, and I don't know where to go for answers other than goggle or YouTube. Yes, I do ask mom and my teachers too.

All I want in life is to earn enough money to take care of myself and family, then buy all types of shoes. I'm in love with all shoes, I can't help it. I don't want to feel ashamed, embarrassed or forced to wear dirty old shoes. Because the one thing that everyone deserves is a good pair of shoes as needed. A pair that covers both feet, not too big or small; a pair that has style, color and compliments any outfit. A pair that makes you feel good inside, a pair that makes you want to smile, and a pair that is just simply the best shoe ever! There are many walks down a long road, dirt or paved, rocky or smooth, maybe wet, or dry; wherever a path takes you let it guide you to your light. You must know yourself and your purpose for life, that's how I walk. I wore my favorite shoes to school one day, had no idea what to expect, and no idea what path I would take when faced with a challenge. We are the chosen ones, mom always say, you are lucky to be human, lucky to be here on earth. My choices will affect my future and if I make them based on morals, values, and ethics the outcome will always be positive. Decisions I make are based on trust, honesty, and positive vibes. .

My family celebrates Kwanzaa, an African American celebration of life. Every year I learn more about my heritage, culture, and myself. My Zawadi, a Swahili word for gift, to family during Kwanzaa will be the gift of shoes. Once a year the family reunites for a cultural celebration of the first fruits. The agricultural harvest festival practiced throughout Africa in December/January. Everyone has a theme gift each year, it's so much fun to give and to receive. I eye gaze at shoes in different places but mainly online. I found a pair of boots that I fell in love with, so I bought them. I think boots will match a lot of my winter wear. Boots are expensive, two hundred sixty-five dollars to be exact. I do have to set a limit on how much or how little I spend. it depends on if they are designer boots. Mom always says, be realistic, don't be greedy, and stay within your budget.

The art of love is to love who you are first and when you do, giving comes naturally. A boy in class comes to school every day without supplies. I'm not sure why but I gave him pens, pencils, paper, journal, calculator, math charts, art supplies, and let him borrow my textbook. I asked my shoe spirit for advice, and wore a favorite pair to class just to deal with that boy. I tell him NO every time he asks the same question. Then one day I snaped and said, "no! I will no longer be accommodating your needs for this classroom, thank you very much". He never spoke to me again, but every once and a while he has the nerve to ask for something and I remain silent. Then he walks to the next victim asking the same question.

My Shoes bring magic to my life so I'm hoping the boots will do the same. I started the school year with new outfits, and managed to buy two pairs of shoes at once. Mom tries her best to make sure we are trending, she knows how important it is for La-La and I. I can't get out of bed; I don't want to go to school, I can't eat, and I feel depressed if I'm not prepared to trend for the new school year. My shoes last year made me feel good inside, gave me confidence about myself. I had a didn't care attitude and I let the haters hate because I had the best shoes collection. Everyone else tells me how much they love my shoes, so they voted them the best shoes of the year. Our school has a yearly contest for social awareness. Students Can win prizes for the best shoes, best dress, best hair style, and best attitude. The reward choices are new shoes and clothes of our choice. Students want to come to school every day because they agree, school is FUN! love school too. The administration team (principal/VPs) creates diversity, artic expression, and educational experiences. The school gives students a chance to thrive with personal leadership. The teachers are kind but firm and motivate students to lead the next generation; by contributing something to the society/world. During the pep really the principal asked the student body, how can she improve the schools environment? What tools are needed to level up learning scores? Students see school as a pipeline to prison because the severity of explosive behaviors, and not complying to rules/expectations. Teenagers are trying to figure out the challenges of growing up in the system as it becomes very difficult when adults get in our way. I tell friends, they can't help the family they were born into; disfigured or disabled, beauty over brains, wealthy or poor, young or old. I am learning to love me just the way I am. Mom says, it could be worse so appreciate your parents and the adults that care.

I hear a lot of students judge others and it comes off as bulling. For whatever reason, exchange communication should be positive instead negative of a tone. I learned not to let words upset me or allow myself to display negative behaviors through aggression. Instead, I practice the art of love with peace and happiness. When all students/people are treated equal no one will feel disrespected or threatened. Everyone will automatically feel popular. All students really want is to be accepted at school. They want others to say hi, when walking by. And when they slip no, one will trip because they had the right fit of a new pair of shoes on. When all students wear their favorite shoes, we become unstoppable. When I wear magic shoes, the mission is to heal students that are hurting. I wave my magic wand and zap some smarts sense into all the girls and boys who think they are better than others. I wonder why that prospective originates in the mind. All the ugly comments and hateful actions will all be zapped away too. When I wear basketball shoes or sneakers, I feel like a superstar! I don't care that I can't read or write or that I'm failing classes. What matters the most is what feeds my ego, running the ball up and down the court. I got kicked off the team because of grades, then found myself in and out of alternative school, but I'm still a VIP. I am more popular now than ever, I'm a bad boy. Who doesn't like a tall, handsome, has plenty of followers and everyone loves me. The truth is, to be accepted by friends I do things that I really don't want to, like hurt people's feelings to guard my own. The chronicles of a student with VIP status. Remember VIP are former or current bullies with negative tendencies.

My father lived with me for the first two years of my life, so I don't know him like I should although I speak to him from a distance. What children need is a two-parent home for emotional balance and stability. Where are all the fathers, and why have they abandoned us. I miss dad and I want him to be around more, to watch me grow, protect me from negative forces and lead me in the right direction in my life. I remember living in Africa as a child for a while, and I hold on to those memories. I remember wearing African shoes for the first time. My feet felt different when walking, and I wondered why. shoes were not too tight and fit my feet just right, but they were very That experience of shoe discomfort led me to believe, I didn't like African shoes. I did overcome my fear during that visit to Sudan, and now I enjoy choosing African fabrics for custom made shoes.

Dad wants to send me a pair of sandals. He tries to make me happy all the way from Africa, I love that about him. I always give him an excuse by saying "you don't have to" because of I'm still a little leery about African shoes. I continue to work through the fears of my feet hurting. I'm learning how to deal with the outcomes of my decisions that lead my actions, simple. This practice will help me become a better person. With social emotional learning in Ms. Su's class, I see the boys are using more positive energy. Learning ways to improve students communication skills make a difference in preframing the mindset. I know that all living things must be nurtured and watered to blossom.

I'm using a symbol of a shoe to make a product line of necklaces to represent life. I'm committed to preparing myself for a future in footwear industry by healing the world one shoe at a time. I enjoy making customize jewelry for the shoe lovers with bold bright colors. I want to earn my fame by offering products and services that help students develop self-awareness through the magic of their shoes. When students participate in a rite of passage, they will receive a necklace (for girls) and bracelet (for boys) after completing the program. The rite of passage is an African tradition that happens when a child reaches puberty at 14. There is a two-week transitional period, which the elders train boys to hunt and provide a guide to manhood. The process for girls is different, there is cooking, sewing, and how to take care of their family. Jewelry is given to signify both groups have completed their duties of cultural awareness, which gives them a new prospective as they reach adulthood at 18. I look forward to a brighter future with much to gain from the Universe.

Teaching a baby how to walk is difficult and parents assume every child will walk according to the charts. Timelines are created to monitor developmental stages and gage progress. I am only fifteen, and no expert on early childhood but the reality is, not all infants follow milestones that are set for them. Human development is an individual progression. A set of twins also have their own identity. The world compares everything to the same standards and laws, sounds like control to the people to me. A baby who sits up weeks before their peers might be the last to crawl. An eighteen-month-old baby that communicates with grunts and gestures suddenly start talking in complete sentences The cycle of life is amazing.

Mom always says, you must walk before you crawl. Parents want to know about potty training, when can babies eat solid food, and other important questions about caring for a child. A child's first steps are big moves toward independence but corrective shoes are necessary for the formation of the feet. Hard sole shoes support weak ankles during developmental stages. What I know so far is walking starts during their first year when coordination of the muscle strengths throughout the body. A baby learns to sit, roll over, and crawl before moving to the next task of pulling up by eight months (according to the timeline). Some babies develop at a faster rate of muscle growth that allows a child to walk. They develop confidence then balance themselves to walk, so without the two skills it can take much longer. The steps of walking are continuous once the baby starts. It's normal for a child to walk at 15 to 17 months old. If the baby takes longer than that I would be a little concerned so call a doctor, they can investigate other factors. A possible delay in walking happens in the brain trying to coordinate the muscle system.

It's important to know how to care for babies/children if you want a babysitting job. Based on research taking a class will provide safety tips, dos and don'ts, schedules for eating, and nap time. A new baby's legs are not strong enough to support their body weight, but if you hold under their arms the legs will dangle as they try to stand. By five months a baby will bounce up and down trying to find a balance. They love bouncing, which is a favorite activity for some time. As the leg muscle continues to develop, the baby masters rolling over, sitting, and crawling. Around eight months pulling up is another milestone that starts, while holding on to anything in sight. After a few weeks of controlling the standing position, the baby is ready to walk. Holding on and moving around until she/he is ready to take off with a fast walk or run. The lesson of life begins with small steps. To summarize the research for my training class, babies need hard sole shoes in the beginning stages of walking. I also present this information to teenage parents, Instead of wearing many hats, I wear many shoes to get the job done. I'm studying health to learn more about human nature and the anatomy. Who we are, and our complex systems. I will teach children about who they are and that All Lives Matter. Most students felt uncomfortable talking about their anatomy however, that changed since social media. Now students love to show their body parts. What they see is what they do whatever is trending. Too many kids are growing up with hood experiences, meaning they are learning life from the streets instead of the foundation of set at home. The Universe is a mystery, we the people are human beings having a spiritual experience and a connection to the cosmos. My spiritual growth comes to me in ways I don't quite expect but I know I am always safe. If I don't understand a topic of discussion, the cosmos and evaluation, I enroll in a class (#outschool) online. The gift of love is… a mom that knows the value of education in small doses, so La-La and I are enrolled in class to learn about how like works through the life cycle. The topics are:

❖ Etymology
❖ History
❖ Evolution
❖ Paleolithic
❖ Transition to civilization
❖ Habitat and population

- ❖ Biology
- ❖ Anatomy
- ❖ Physiology
- ❖ Genetics
- ❖ Life cycle
- ❖ Race and ethnicity
- ❖ Diet
- ❖ Sleep
- ❖ Psychology
- ❖ Consciousness and thought
- ❖ Motivation and emotion
- ❖ Society and culture
- ❖ Sexuality and love
- ❖ Gender roles
- ❖ Society, government, and politics
- ❖ Trade and economics
- ❖ War
- ❖ Material culture and technology
- ❖ Language
- ❖ Spirituality and religion
- ❖ Philosophy and self-reflection
- ❖ Science and mathematics
- ❖ Art

Everyone can make a difference when they discover their natural passion. Passon is energy, and to feel the energy that comes from focusing on what excites you is power. When we find our passion, we can discover ourselves. And, what what pair of shoes will lead the way? One sunny morning I walked on the beach to meditate and see the sun rise. I stepped over debris that washed ashore after a storm including small fish, yuck! I picked up garbage and other and a little seaweed, I was prepared with PPE. I told my friends to help clean the beach for our community service. Of course, they didn't want to by saying, "No let someone else clean it up, we on vacation". I looked them with a glare and said, "Try save the Earth one step at a time, and this the time". I handed them a set of PPE. How would the shoes fit if I don't encourage others to do something about the beach environment, while on vacation? I enjoy participating and volunteering in events that serves others; young or old, rich or poor, black or white, family or not I focus on kind being kind to others, staying close to family, and when I finally make my escape into the world; I will make a life for myself. When I graduate from high school, I'm seeking higher education to give myself a head start in life. I want a new life with a new set of rules, my own.

My community service continues with visiting senior citizen homes during summer break. This population are often neglected so they need love and support too. When you help others, you are indirectly helping yourself; in ways you don't realize. I made a list of all things that serve the community and unite people together to share with my friends. Mom encourages her daughters to be successful in life, which has nothing to do with how much money is in your pocket. Mom says, "blessed are those who can give without remembering, and take without forgetting. When I put on my magic shoes I can commit to change.

Mom speaks in quotes, something she inherited from her parents. One day she spoke her language all day to make a point. First, many people will walk in and out of your life, but only true friends and family will leave footprints in your heart. Then mom said , "When you were born you cried and the world rejoiced, live your life so that when you die, the world continues to cry and rejoice over you". When my aunt passed away, I stood in front of family and friends with my red shoes on and recited that same quote. I don't what my future holds but I'm scared, frighten, and worried about many things. There are many things that can't be explained, so live your best life today. They come and go; don't say you know if you haven't walked in my shoes. Forgive me for the things I do, being mean comes from being green #mybirthmark. Try walking in my shoes, a journey of a thousand miles begins with a single step.

A Shoe Book

My English teacher tells me to always visualize the subject in a story. I do a lot of journaling and creating vision boards, it's a way of self-expression. Anger must be channeled with the forces from within. Writing is not a bad idea I tell my friends and the VIPs. Write it down I tell them. I journal a lot, it's how I speak my emotions and focus on my self-care. I love reading, researching, and writing, so I blog about people, places, and things; good and bad. I realized that writing is magical because one day I had this thought that turned into an idea then a project. My passion for shoes and writing led me to get hired to blog. The topics or themes starts with a story or article, and I summarize it. I write about? Things that may affect the outcomes in life, the lives I just use my imagination when writing anything, always adding a little sparkle to plan a perfect life. I would like to help others by teaching how to plan and organize their lives. Everybody knows everything in this digital era and refuse to practice the art of listening. For a middle school student, I must think about high school and grow up. I must start making decisions without mom, that's a little scary. I must rely on the knowledge and lessons she gave me. Going to college or a training institution will give me the structure I will need for life, and financial freedom. I'm just trying to get to my destiny, not too fast but not too slow, time is wasted if you don't know. My shoe book is about life as we know it, scenarios in the shoe world. I've collected children's books for my research that are written with a basic theme, shoes of course. My story is about the personalities, IQs, and a love of life as a future wife. When I use my imaginary vision, I can see clearly what's in front of me; one step at a time.

My Feet got bigger from heel to toe. Time for new shoes so off we go!
Shoes that zip up and shoes that tie,
Shoes to tiptoe to the sky, Shoes that clatter and shoes that clop, Shoes that light up when I hop.

Shoe Baby

In a shoe you might think there is not much to do, but the shoe becomes a boat to sail away in or a car going to the zoo. For the baby sitting in a red shoe, she drives it like a car, flies it like a plane, and arrives just in time for tea.

African King and Queen shoes looks fun, but they belong to mom and dad and I magically shrunk inside the shoe. But when baby steps out of the shoe, she's back to normal size. So glad for that mom who thought her child was gone.

Shoes For Me

Hippo's feet have grown! She's off to the store where mom lets her choose her very own shoes. Hippo tries on every pair until she steps, being careful not to fall. steps when she walk being real careful not to fall.

Hello Shoes

A simple story of a boy and his grandfather looking for a missing sandals. Grandpa takes them off wherever he goes, then expects someone else to find them. After they are found the boy is happy, now he can figure out how to put on his difficult shoes all by himself.

A Flock of Shoes

South she doesn't want them anyway, so she learns to love her winter south. She doesn't want them anyway, so she learns to love her winter boots instead. Then one day her boots heard a sound walking north, so they jumped on board and now they are missing too.

Shoes

A little girl that counts her feet and toes decides to give away a pair of shoes and socks. The girl encourages everyone to donate a pair of shoes as she learns to give unconditionally.

Those Shoes

An important issue is raised when a decision must to be made, is it a want or a need. Shoelaces must be tied independently. Learning how to tie shoes is difficult no doubt. Using a a step-by-step color illustration with a huge wooden shoe is a tool we use the laced model shoe has the components of a real one that challenges the hand-eye coordination.

Birdie's Big-Girl Shoes

Little B can't wait to be like her mom, and will can't wait until she's grown. She loves wearing jewelry, spritzing perfume, and dressing up in front of the mirror. But more than anything, Birdie fantasizes about her mother's fancy high-heels and can't wait to try them on. Where will she go? Just walking around with those big-girl shoes on.

Do Princesses Wear Hiking Boots

Every girl wonders about being a real Princess. Nyla has energetic thrust and a very smart child. Her level of questioning is important and needs to be answered. Can Princesses ride tricycles, climb trees, do chores, or eat the crusts of bread for a snack? Her mother's voice is reassuring as she answers her daughter's concerns. By telling her a Princess has high self-esteem and is very confident. A gentle lesson about self-acceptance will inspire children to follow their dreams.

Stink has the Worst Super-Stinky Sneakers

Omar's nickname is stinky and not because he stinks. His second-grade class went on a field trip to the Science Museum. A new exhibit called, Gross Me-Out; The Science of Smells. Stinky discovered that his nose sensory has amazing abilities. He becomes preoccupied with the smells from: used toilet water, dead flowers water, and extreme smells from vomit, a decaying body, diarrhea and more. So, he voted on which smell was the absolute worst for him. I was shocked when choose the rotten smelly sneakers. It was foul enough to win the Golden Shoe Award.

New Red Shoes

A young girl name Dee goes shopping for shoes. She was allowed to buy her favorite pair. So, Dee gets shiny red shoes for a friends birthday party. She was so excited about wearing the new shoes and decided to buy a second pair of the same shoes for a friend. Sharing is caring.

Two Shoes, New Shoes

Two nursery books featuring two toddlers learning the concepts of color, shape, and sizes. This is an early start to fundamental skills of sorting and matching. This engagement keeps toddlers focus on the task.

The Story of Grump & Pout

A human comes to the forest and sells custom-made shoes to the Monsters. They have very large feet, so custom made shoes is a big relief to aching feet. Monster Grump stopped his grumps and Monster Pout no longer pouts. Both Monsters are learning to change their grumpy behaviors.

The Blue Shoe: A Tale of Thievery, Villainy, Sorcery, and Shoes

Manu Kingsly is sitting in jail, wondering why he failed in life. His blue shoe was ruined and someone he was helping is now missing, and he's facing robbery charges. Manu will be deported to the far side of Mt. Zexnax in the morning, "and that's where he shall get the help he needs," said the officer. He might find that missing girl, or maybe rescue his mother from uncertainty. No one has ever returned from Mt. Zexnax, so perhaps Manu is optimistic to be dreaming of a rescue. Then again, he is a dreamer, a doer, and a thief. He is the type of boy who would challenge the mountain and escape.

Shoe-La-La!

Lashoe is her name, but she calls herself shoe La-La. She brings Friend's home to meet the family. Then all went to a shoe store to look for the perfect pair. With so many shoes, the girls froze with excitement. They are now ready to attend the shoe expedition with their light-up boots. Boots with zippers, straps, buckles, and feathers. How about glitter a little bit of glue, and don't forget the leather and tap boots. The girls have a LOT of Imagination and had best boots on.

Lucy and the La-Di-Da Shoes

Every girl wants a pair of sparkly, shiny, lacey, and pretty La-Di-Da shoes that bring out her best. Lucy's mother doesn't see the good she has. That's because Lucy will only wear the brown tie-up shoes. almost every day. But when her best friend Dolly comes to school with shiny new sparkly shoes that glow, Lucy wants a pair of her own, something sparked her interested in her shoe ware. She learns the bonds of friendship greater than shoe envy.

The Shoe Family Lessons

In life you get all dressed up and forget to wear your shoes

I have aways dreamed of having a family; a husband, four kids, a dog, and white picket fence. I'm starting to understand why life lessons are taught at an early age. These lessons are needed before I become an adult. I treasure everything mom said in a simple quote. Magic shoes can be found all around the world, and everyone has a pair but don't know it. The Shoe Family could be a model of my life as an adult. Married with a bunch of kids when I only wanted four (2-boys and 2-girls). A good staple home with organization, a value/belief/ rules system, I believe it refines the purpose of family. I will teach my family life lessons the way my mother taught her children. I sure this imaginary life has problems too, but I hope not as intense as real one. I will raise my children in a holistic way, teaching them how to ground themselves. How to be strong, helpful, independent, and peaceful. Teach them all they need to know to navigate the world systems and win. We will love all each child equally to feel their spirit, and give them our very best as parents, and it comes with sacrifices. The life lessons for my futuristic children are of course; standards, tradition, and spiritual awareness. These lessons will be practice every day for character building. I hope the world is a better place when I grow up. A world that is fair to all people regardless of who you are, where you live, how you look, what color shoes you wear, or how much money you have. I hope a married life takes me on a journey where I want to go.

Monday

It's Monday morning time for everyone in the house to wake up. It's going to be a busy week. We are Mr. and Mrs. Shoe, with a family of 15 children. The names are *Shoe Baby, Shoes For Me, Hello Shoes, Flock of Shoes, Those Shoes, Bride's Big girl Shoes, Princesses Hiking Boots, Stinky Sneakers, New Red Shoes, Two New Shoes, Grump and Pout, The Blue Shoe, Shoe La-La, and Lucy's La-Di-Da Shoes.* We know who they are from their descriptions before we adopted them. With this big family an organizational system is a must, so we have that in place. With a digital daily communication board, there is one displayed in every room. People always ask, how do we keep up with so many children I reply, "with structure of course". What keeps our family going is the love of shoes. Mr. Shoe and I have a retail shoe store with other closet items for sale. we sell. We have a large customer base due to our concept of a shoe We have unique ways of advertising. The children range from tots to teens, and we teach them what they need to survive. The most successful people in the world are happy because they love who they are. And they always keep themselves busy doing what they love. Mr. Shoe and I will film a journey of our family dynamics in just one week, so Lights, camara, action.

OUR DAILY ROUTINE SCHEDULE

Shoe Baby and *Two Shoes/New Shoes* are my three toddlers and they are the first group to get up every morning. Everyone's clothes are laid out before going to bed in their custom built closets. Clothes and shoes are coordinated by color. The idea is for the kids to grab and go. We match outfits with shoes as an easy step for this group. Our family relies on a visual color system with a digital schedule. The structure at home is extremely important. The entire family depends on a strict schedule during the week. Our rigorous lifestyle helps with the development of analytical thinking skills. The house was built to accommodate our family. Each room has two full size beds, and large closets. There are 10 bedrooms, a large game room, library, art/crafts room, and a home theater. The backyard has a playground, pool, basketball, and tennis courts. *Shoe Baby loves* to hide inside her big shoe car then takes off only to crash into everything. She has a shoe bed that shakes, spends, and takes off ready to fly. The tots are amazing. *Two Shoes/New Shoes* enjoy learning concepts of patterns and shapes using colored manipulatives with lots of pieces to keeps them busy. I get them all dressed up then down the stairs we go for breakfast before the next group wakes up. I put the toddlers in the game and main room, that's where they stay until it's time to go.

The next group to awake are the girls, they take longer to get dressed and get downstairs. We have eight girls, so I brush their hair in a ponytail if it's not braided. Six of the girls can dress themselves making the process for this group faster. We have double sinks in each bathroom, line move faster. The girls know there's no time to play in the morning. *Flock of Shoes* are always migrating in places other than her closet, where shoes belong. Her sandals often fly away to join other flocks. Durning winter her boots take the train heading north for the season. *Flock of Shoes* digital schedule shows the footwear for the day. So, she refuses and makes her own choice. Now Those Shoes is a different kind of girl. Her feet are growing too fast, and she's happy with wearing the on pair that fits every day. Shoe *La-La* loves the color of all shoes and follow the schedule for what she will wear. But she still picks out her own pair each night, I just smile because it makes her happy. Her shoes have zippers, straps, buckles, and taps.

New Red Shoes talked about going to a birthday party for a long time, and now it's time. I'm taking her today to buy new shoes for the party. Her new shoe choice is always red and refuses to wear any other color. Birdie's Big Girl Shoes want to be just like her mom, so she hangs out in my closet watching my every move. Always in front of a mirror looking at herself in my clothes, jewelry, and shoes Princesses Hiking Boots is inquisitive and really wants to be a Princess. She wears her crown every day, and ask lots of questions about hiking boots. She doesn't understand that Princesses don't wear hiking boots. We found a nice pair of boots (we call all her shoes boots) to dress up her shoe collection to more elegant styles for a Princess. Shoes For Me is called Hippo because she walks like one, and it takes her forever to decide about what shoes to wear. I choose what's best for her feet and she agrees with a bit of attitude. All the girls have different tastes in footwear, and very particular about their shoes. It's time for the girls to head downstairs..

The Boys will be the last group to wake up because they are much faster to get downstairs. Mr. Shoe handles this group while I'm putting lunches together. I have concerns for the boys, and Mr. Shoe is working to find solutions while they are still young. *Blue Shoe* seems to get in trouble and I'm not sure why. His decision-making skill are Confusing, and leads to bad choices. Blue honestly tries to help people but always manage to get himself in trouble instead. He is not a thief, that I know of, because I never caught him stealing. He enjoys imagery play, like going in and out of space galaxies and trapped on Mt. Zexnax. Grump is always pouting and grumpy about everything, we need to find out why. I see him in the backyard every day talking to the trees, or the Universe. He believes the only way to stop pouting about nothing is to sell custom made shoes to his forest friends. He keeps himself busy by making shoes out of construction paper and cardboard for his friends in the forest. Stinky is a boy that loves grossed out smelly stuff. This boy has been grossed out and stinky since the day he arrived. He loves Science, digging for worms, and anything that smells horrible. Hello Shoes, is always looking for his sandals, which is the only shoes he will wear; they are his favorite. He knows the rules about taking shoes off and where to place them. Grandpa always clean up the mess Hello Shoes leaves everywhere. When he looks for his sandals, he finds them and it makes him very happy. Boys will be boys and they all pretty much swallow breakfast in one bite. Then everyone lineup at the door and wait for their bus to arrive.

The house was designed to have the bedrooms upstairs with theme rooms down stairs. All the children take the school bus except the toddlers. Mr. Shoe is out the door after the boy's finish breakfast, and off to work at out Shoe Closet Store. The store hours: 9am to 9pm, Monday thru Saturday and closed on Sunday. The retail business requires long hours to serve our customers. Therefore, we hire different family services to meet the needs of our children. Such as, a Buddhist Monk that comes to our home on Sunday's. A cleaning service to meet our daily needs, a choir once a month for music lessons, and a daily chef, and a babysitter as needed. Sunday is the one day of the week that Mr. Shoe and do not leave our room for entire day. No one is allowed to knock on the door or ask us any questions by standing at our door. In fact, we do not speak to the children at all. The sitter will send a text message for emergencies only. On Monday's there are no after school activities planned and we update the digital schedule boards for the week. It's time to get on the bus, it takes three buses to get everyone to school. The district recognizes our unique family needs with student pick up at the house, and other personal care services. The school helps us manage the biggest family in the district. First the elementary bus arrives and I always count the kids leaving with my checklist. Then comes the middle then finally the high school bus. What a relief when the house is almost empty but quiet. I go upstairs with the three toddlers and get dress for work.

I am finally out the door, headed to daycare a few doors from the Shoe Closet Store. We have two part time employees and senior citizens who love to volunteer when they can. This store gives me a purpose to fulfill my desire, giving everyone the magic of shoes. The rewards I received from my shoes as a teenager, allows me to share it with the world through the Shoe Closet Store. My first pair to shoes, was the pair that changed my life. It sits on a glass shelf in the store. As customers walk in, they see a message board that reads; welcome to the Closet. Posted round the store we have shoe collages and FYI (for your information) boards of shoe facts and current sales. The kids loved cutting out pictures of boots, pumps, sandals, sneakers, slippers, work shoes, bare feet, and anything that belongs on the foot; just like I did when I was in middle school. When I met Mr. Shoe in college I fell in love with his shoes first. It was St. Patrick's Day, he was wearing the coolest glittery green sneakers with a hat to match. I thought he was a Leprechaun; the kids laugh every time I tell that story. My husband is from Ghana, West Africa but he said his great, great, great grandmother was an Irish woman. He always honors her life by dressing up on St. Patrick's Day. I am so lucky to have a friend and partner who knows exactly want he wants out of life, and take the steps through action to get it. When we first met, we shared similar stories. Our goals were compatible especially for shoes, children and business adventures.

THINGS TO DO TODAY

Date_____   COMPLETED

1) _____ ☐
2) _____ ☐
3) _____ ☐
4) _____ ☐
5) _____ ☐
6) _____ ☐
7) _____ ☐
8) _____ ☐
9) _____ ☐
10) _____ ☐

School ends at 3:00pm for elementary and 4:00pm for middle and high school. I work the sales floor with the employees and volunteers, while Mr. Shoe is completing the, To Do List. On Saturday's the older children work in the store for Experience in the real world and managing the family business. We created a family room in the back of the store, equipped with gaming options that has everyone's favorite systems and electronics. Also, a desktop, laptops (PCs/MACs), and printer for last minute school assignments. There is cyber security in place for the internet safety protocols. The worldwide web is a place of negative energy and should not be available to children without supervision. I leave work at 3:00pm every day for parent pick up of the toddlers then get home before the first bus arrive. I display "What's for Dinner" on the board, and the menu for the week on Mondays. I am training the everyone to use less verbal and more nonverbal communication. Simply by looking at the boards first, then answer their own questions during peak hours, and stressful times. With an emoji to indicate the mood at the current moment. When everyone gets off the bus, they go straight into the family room to meditate. I understand school is difficult, it's the system. No one is allowed upstairs before dinner, that's a rule. The family room is divided into sections for a guest bedroom with a full bathroom. So, this is where it all happens after school. A park in the backyard is right off the kitchen so I can see everyone when I'm busy assembling dinner plates. Dinner time is 5:30pm sharp and once the menu is posted there are no substitutes. After dinner is homework and study time for one hour. Then kitchen duties are listed for those over ten twice a week. My kitchen duties as a child started at 8 years old.

At 7:30pm the first group head upstairs to prepare for the evening routines, which consists of the shower/hygiene's process. Then choosing outfits and shoes (for approval). Then Ironing once the outfit inspected. I do a nightly closet checks in each room to make sure everyone is compliant with a check done On their boards. Then I say a prayer in each room and let the kids use their words to talk about the Universe. With a kiss good night, lights out and doors shut. Lights Out at 8:30pm no exceptions. This entire process takes one hour between rotations. I like to read bedtime stories after prayer on scheduled days, it's always fun with the boys. On Sundays we ask the children about their dreams and passions. And what they want to do in life or add to the world when they grow up. That's so important to have conversations about world history. It's natural to hear what the children have to say about life, the world and what future holds. It makes my heart smile. There are no problems during bedtime routines. Research shows, when the body (young and old) get at least eight hours of rest the brain allows all systems to function properly. Mr. Shoe gets home by 9:30pm and we're fast to sleep by 10:00pm.

Tuesday

Good Morning Sunshine… The alarm is going off and babies are crying, it's time to get up. The morning routine starts by checking the board for today's schedule. I must take La-Di-Da *to* the mall to buy new shoes. Her dull brown shoes she loves so much must be replaced. We are replacing the old shoes with the same style and encouraging different colors instead of just brown. Tuesdays, Thursdays, and Sunday's the hired help for house comes in for cleaning services. Mr. Shoe and I get the babies dressed and send them downstairs with the babysitter before I wake up the other two groups. I must become a drill sergeant during morning duties, and I do it in a loving way. Mr. Shoe and I are role models, teaching the family about time management. This process is to decrease the amount of time spent on a specific task. I'm hoping to increase their efficiency to complete tasks. Teaching children how to manage their time helps them become aware of how much time is wasted when you don't keep track of it. Time management helps with tasks to get completed faster, schoolwork, chores, and goals to accomplish in life. Also, organization is another time management skills to develop. The family will work on those skills first then we will discuss again, respecting rules and laws at home and community. Today we are taking inventory in the store to prepare for the new season. That requires organizational skills to sell out the old inventory and prepare for new seasonal merchandise. Our sales are increasing daily as we are seeing growth patterns, especially in the shoe department. When customers buy footwear, we offer a clothing discount. A strategy to increase sales.

I'm leaving the store at 2:30pm today, picking up *La-Di* Da from school then heading to the mall. She wants of pretty shoes for a school party. That's a miracle for her, the girl that only wears the same old shoes. She picked out a pair of sparkly, shiny, and pretty brown shoes for the party. I convinced her to try another color, she agreed on green to match her dress. She only wants to prove to others that she has magic shoes too. I picked up the babies at 6:00pm and head home, slightly off schedule. Although I know that, everything is fine at home, I worry because I'm not there. That's when I do my breathing meditation to calm down. When I walked in the house everyone's in place; the house is peaceful, clean, and dinner is completed. The kitchen is clean and there were no attempts to go upstairs. Tonight, Stinky Sneakers will make a presentation about his science project and everyone will help him. We have group projects to work together or collaborate for time management. Stinky Sneakers enters the Science Fair every year because he loves stenches, and the worst smells ever. He wants to create a foul odor that is sure to stink up a room. With a dozen of dead flowers. This idea is to let the flowers sit in the same water for thirty days, then pour that water in a sealed jar. Everyone agrees that it's a great idea and will make the top 10 project. I dismissed everyone from the family den to head upstairs. Since Grandpa is over to spend time, everyone will get ready for bed then come back downstairs. Grandpa always read books to the children from our library. He reads his favorite bedtime stories and make everyone happy. After grandpa finished, he took group one upstairs for bed. I will have a presentation of a topic to discuss. As parents it's important that we have the conversations thatt make teens feel uncomfortable. Like the birds and bees, or male and female identity. Tonight start a six-part series of health and wellness education. Mr. Shoe and I will take turns then both come together as a family for part-six to summarize the training and set expectations. The traditional role of a man and a woman looks different in every culture. With a set of rules passed down by ancestors. Posted on the activity board is a list of fun things to do for teens. This is how to keep teenagers busy from distractions of society. Using analytical thinking skills, creates constructive ideas that are critical for decision making.

Alternative Choices For Teen Play

1. Go to the movies with your friends/family.

2. Go shopping at the mall with your friends.

3. Have a picnic with your friends at a local park or in your backyard.

4. Have an 80's movie marathon. Rent as many 80's movies as you can find and watch them all in one weekend. Do the same thing for other decades.

5. Make a scrapbook.

6. Make a collage that represents you or a topic you enjoy. Include magazine and newspaper clippings, photographs, ticket stubs, etc.

7. Have a potluck dinner. Assign a food category to each of your friends and set a date.

8. Read a book or magazine.

9. Play a game of flag or touch football.

10. Make a home movie with your parent's video camera, or iPhone.

11. Paint a picture.

12. Go on a scavenger hunt in your neighborhood.

13. Go to a school football or basketball game.

14. Start a collection of something

15. Play a game of Frisbee.

16. Go swimming.

17. Make a mix CD.

18. Organize a bake sale or car wash in your neighborhood, and donate the proceeds to an organization.

19. Play cards or dominoes.

20. Plan and make a meal for your family.

22. Make your own waterslide. Put a plastic tarp down on the grass and wet it down with a water hose. Keep the hose running as you and your friends run and slide.

22. Fly a kite in your backyard or at a local park.

23. Create your own street-hockey team or play for fun.

24. Talk on the phone.

25. Ride your bike. Try to find new trails.

26. Write poetry or short stories.

27. Build a clubhouse in your backyard where you can hang out with your friends.

28. Make homemade cookies.

29. Go on a photography hunt and find interesting themes to shoot.

30. Exercise. Try new exercise routines with your friends, such as yoga or Pilates.

31. Rent a canoe or paddle boat.

32. Go to a concert.

33. Start your own band.

34. Get a part-time job.

35. Go out to eat at a local restaurant.

36. Go to an ice cream shop with your friends.

37. Go star-gazing.

38. Go see a play at your local theater or a school production.

39. Participate in after-school activities, such as the drama club, football, basketball, community service clubs, student council, cheerleading, etc.

40. Go to a museum.

41. Go to the zoo.

42. Volunteer at the local animal shelter, hospital, nursing home or another place that interests you.

43. Plant your own garden or terrarium.

44. Make a time capsule with all your friends with notes and objects you want to remember this time in history. Set a date to open it far in the future.

45. Design and make your own T-shirts.

46. Go horseback riding.

47. Go rock climbing or hiking.

48. Go to an amusement or water park.

49. Have dinner outside while watching the sunset. You can make dinner or pick up some fast food.

50. Groom your pet then take him to the park to show him off.

51. Play paintball.

52. Go to the beach or lake.

53. Play computer/video games for a game night.

54. Take a nap.

55. Play laser tag.

56. Play miniature golf.

57. Ride go-carts.

58. Go bowling.

59. Study for SATs.

60. Go to a flea market to search for cool stuff.

61. Order a pizza and rent a movie with your friends.

62. Attend a professional sporting event.

63. Go ice-skating.

64. Visit public gardens.

65. Play board games with your little brother or sister or with your friends.

66. Learn how to play a musical instrument.

67. Take your sisters or brothers to a movie.

68. Take your sisters or brothers to a playground or circus.

69. Visit the historical sites of your city.

70. Start a recycling program in your school/community.

71. Have a poker party. Use chips, candy and pretzels instead of money.

72. Make a music video.

73. Make a present for your boyfriend or girlfriend.

74. Make a quilt out of your old T-shirts and blankets.

75. Have a cartoon marathon.

76. Go roller-skating or roller-blading at the local skating rink or around the neighborhood.

77. Go to the batting cages or play baseball in a local park.

78. Take a blanket and some snacks to a park and look at cloud formations in the sky.

79. Listen to music/sing.

80. Start a daily journal.

81. Put together a play production with your friends.

82. Roast marshmallows.

83. Play catch with water balloons in the yard, or have a water balloon fight.

84. Visit your family.

85. Do a puzzle. Glue the pieces together and frame it.

86. Organize a garage sale with your friends. Donate the proceeds to a local charity or throw a party.

87. Build your own website.

88. Go fishing.

89. Surf the Internet.

90. Take dance lessons. Learn how to swing dance, waltz, salsa, etc.

91. Organize a day to pick up litter in your neighborhood and in the community.

92. Go to the library.

93. Study something new.

94. Write a letter.

95. Rearrange your room.

96. Clean out the basement or garage for your parents.

97. Mow the lawn or wash car for your parents.

98. Mentor a younger child.

99. Join a club or group.

100. Take cooking classes.

101. Visit a nursing home.

Blue Shoe has something to tell, I know it's about school; Ok, I tell him. Before lights goes off, I sit with him in my room to talk. He started with telling a story about his friend Nick. How he hurts himself by showing self-injurious behaviors. His girlfriend broke up with him on Facebook live. He was so mad he grabbed a knife and made harmful attempts of hurt. I asked *Blue Shoe* if his parents knew, and where did it happen before? "At his house, but no one knows but me". Nick told *Blue Shoes* His mother doesn't care, he doesn't see her for days at a time. His mother works the night shift. This kid needs help, so I asked *Blue Shoe* if he has a cell phone or knows where he lives. If I can help a parent with a troubled child, I will do everything possible to intervene. When kids are emotionally troubled, parents are the last to know and sometimes late. Teen depression is associated with many factors including being bullied, frustrated, and angry.

Parents especially teens and new mothers are offered parenting classes before leaving the hospital. There are no instructional manuals, no license required to raise a child. So, educational workshops on parenting in high schools are beneficial for teens make better choices. Each one, teach one, mom always said and now I use that same quote with my family. Early warning signs of a child in distress should be noted. Children must know that parents are concerned about their well-being, safety, and happiness.

In African culture, it takes a village to raise a child. The traditional nuclear family consist of two parents and children. Not all families are nuclear, single parent families out-weigh traditional standards. Therefore, kids in trouble need the support of family. If the family is broken the community must become involved. Parents need places to speak out and speak up to get help and information. I talked to Nick's mother and offered resources that could help his behavior. At least try to get to the root of his problem, she agreed. A boarding school, residential treatment center, or camping in mountains or lake are some things that can help him. This is a good place to start the healing process for teens. For any teenager sitting in a cell, wondering what happened and how they got there, it's too late. Sometimes teens in trouble need a space to feel safe when they are hurting inside.

Wednesday

Today I wake up tired, I check the Wednesday schedule. It's sports Night Ok another busy day. It's quiet, and the sound of silence is peaceful. I do a spot check in all the room closets. In Flock of Shoes closet, she doesn't have a complete outfit ready. Her shoes must have flown off again because they are missing. I'm back in my room and hear a noise in my closet. I opened the door and smiled at Flock of Shoes with my clothes on, and her missing shoes. Mr. Shoe gets up and we start the schedule, the morning routines. Everyone seems balanced on a Wednesday's, maybe they finally listening. Or they don't' want me to shout, "is anyone listening". New Shoes, Red Shoes have a party tonight, birthdays must be celebrated on a school night. All groups ate a breakfast bar, fruit, and water for a quick morning snack.

I give out lunch bags to put in backpacks, let's hope they all make it in. Busses come and go and off to work I go. Sometimes I feel an enormous amount of pressure and responsibility as a mom. This family life is overwhelming, I appreciate the involvement from my partner Mr. Shoe especially on Wednesdays. I meditate all day to release stress and anxiety, and give all my worries to the Universe first thing in the morning. I love having a business and working at the store, it gives me a purpose and allows me to feel liberated. I wished for a large family and I got it. I remember my mom always said, be careful what you wish for because you might just get it. Mr. Shoe and I don't get many date nights out, so we create our own version at home. Once a month is a requirement to plan an activity outside the house. It's important of our mental health. Relaxing the body is an important step to wellness with daily practice.

- Taking slow deep breaths help release stress in the body. When I'm stressed I breathe in and out to help me feel clam. Thinking of good things is a simple way to lower stress levels immediately like how wonderful my kids are, and the greatest vacation ever!

- Changing my attitude to think positive about situations and outcomes, instead of being worried about what I didn't get done. I think about what I did accomplish on the to do list.

- Let it go, sometimes I just have to recognize I can't change the world but I can change situations that I control, myself and my family.

- Taking a small mental break will remove me from the environment by closing my eyes, giving myself a moment to reflect before taking on another task.

- I try to exercise every day, even ten minutes of stretches, jumping in place, and deep breathing is better than nothing at all. A good workout each week can release anxiety and to balance myself.

- I find time for hobbies like scrapbooking, vision boards, baking, gardening, crafts, reading, swimming, or playing a musical instrument. Finding time to turn away from work by giving myself short breaks between tasks before going back to work.

- Getting away from my family, away from bill due dates, away from chores and errands to spend time with myself.

- Laugher is needed in heavy doses whether it's from someone telling a joke, watching a funny movie, listening to a comedian, or even laughing at a senseless reality show it releases silent stress.

Today was a good day after all, although I was feeling a little stressed I was able to make myself feel better as the day went on. Getting my happiness back is not only important for me but for my family. Mr. Shoe and switch schedules on Wednesday's due game night. I pick up the toddlers and pizza, then drop off children and food at home; returned to the store until closing. Game night starts at 5:00pm, The children are allowed to invite their friends that comes with parent volunteers. Which is necessary due to the number of families that show up. Up to forty people in and outside the house. It's always a late night on Wednesdays but a fun night of competition games, eating pizza, and entertainment. Everyone is tired and ready for bed, they make it up stairs by 9:00pm. So, no bedtime stories on Wednesday nights. Lights out by 10:00pm.

Thursday

Mr. Shoe gets up first, does all the closet checks that didn't happened last night. We are reversing roles today, so I'm out the door early this morning. A parent training class is scheduled today at the store, along with the final planning of a children's fashion on Saturday. The To Do List today is a long one. I will meet with the sponsors to provide the clothing lines. I ordered flyers for the store and posted the event on social media. But first the training class, which includes social skills topics and subtopics. I do understand discipline is difficult for parents when applying routines and providing structure in the home. It takes daily practice teaching fundamental skills to children. Discipline is the practice of training children to obey the expectations of behaviors. That can be a list of rules and the consequences when the child doesn't follow them. Discipline promotes the ability to recognize and change negative behaviors. This training is for both children and adults. The workshops are once a month on Saturdays. We are starting to see a lot of parents attend regularly based on their needs and wants. Today I will host the meeting but there are different presenters each month. Today twenty-five parents including fathers registered. I'm happy to see parents getting involved. Parents are the key to positive outcomes for children, teens, and adults. I provide a list of effective discipline techniques, and explain each one by answering questions. I use hands on projects, visual strategies, and video clips to keep parents engage. I ask parents for feedback at the end of session. Children can slowly understand their actions that lead to the start of change. Children really want to be good by nature but struggle to maintain obedience. Teenagers have issues with authority figures that always lead to trouble with the police.

Parent Questions

- Why is my son always forgetting things?
- Does my child participate in the classroom activities?
- Do I expect too much when I ask my teenager to watch her little sister?
- Can my child in 1st grade follow rules?
- How will I know my son is being bullied or bulling others?
- How do I know if my child is getting the attention he needs?
- Can my daughter be reacting to negative behaviors?
- What are the signs of depression in teens?

Tips for Preventing Misbehavior

Provide Love and Affection at Home... Increase the number of hugs you give your children. Tell them they are loved and spend more time to create a bond. Children need to know they are loved and safe, especially ones with know that parents care for them and gives them structure have less behavior problems. Sometimes they can misbehave to get parents attention however, when parents are present children are likely to obey.

Encourage Good Behavior... Children need to feel important. Helping parents with family task makes children feel important and valued. Thank your children for helping you and let them know how they have contributed to the family.

Arrange the Environment... School age children are learning to do more themselves. For example, they may want to get their own snacks after school or make dinner for the family. Place paper cups and plates in their reach. Buy small containers of juice that are easy for children to drink. You can also prevent your kids from munching on junk food after school by stocking your kitchen with healthy snacks.

Provide Positive Choices... Keep children engaged in interactive educational activities over redundant material or electronics. give them a chance to think. For example, set a limited on watching television then turn it off when the show is over. Allow the child to ride on his/her bike or play a game. Ask children what they would like to do then offer a choice.

Whenever possible, keep routines consistent... Children gain a sense of security and trust through daily routines. They can be upset by sudden change, so prepare them in advance about what will happen in the future and why. Let them know what to expect for example, if you cancel a trip explain why, then ask your children to suggest another day.

Set Realistic Rules of Behavior... This involves setting rules that match children's physical development (hand-eye coordination, strength), mental skills (attention span, memory), and social skills (ability to share and understand the feelings of others). The expectations and rules set for younger children will differ for teens. They can remember the steps in setting the dinner table, or caring for the family dog. Helping with chores at home gives children (younger and older) a sense of belonging and builds confidence.

Examine the Need for a Rule... Rules exist for reasons children don't understand. They exist to protect children, adults, and even animals. Rules help children get along with other people for other cultures.

They also protect personal belongings too. Children have difficulty remembering lots of rules at once. So, have five important rules and consistently enforce them..

Explain the reason for the rule... Children are more likely to follow a rule when they understand why the rule exists. Be sure to tell them the reason. With understanding children can remember to act their best when adults are not around.

This class was great! I used the tips at home and they work, giving real strategies that's been tried and tested. After the workshop, customers typically look around the store for items to buy. We always have sales items available giving customers a reason shop. Today was just one class scheduled instead of two, it depends on the enrollment. For Saturday's event I'm using ten models, For the fashion preview. Tomorrow is dress rehearsal with the models. *La-La* is flying in town for the big event. I haven't seen her and the girls in while, so I'm glad she's coming to help. *La-La* has two children of her own now, I named Shoe *La-La* after her. The fashion review will take an hour. Tomorrow we will select the garments, separate them by style, theme, and size. The garments will be sold before and after the two shows on Saturday, two thousand pieces for sale. When I get home there is peace and serenity because everyone is asleep. Mr. Shoe does a great job caring for his children in my absence. Dinner waiting and I am hungry! Then we head to the theater for a movie. Nice but I'm too tired for that so I head upstairs to bed.

Friday

Morning Glory! I give praise to the Universe every single morning especially on Fridays. I asked Mr. Shoe if we can switch places toady, his schedule is far less stressful. Everyone that's in the fashion review are out of school today. There's a lot to do in preparation for Saturday. This morning I introduced an activity called, "I'm thankful for, and wanted the children to think about that phase today. We will continue it after school today for a Friday night party. Everyone will meet up in the family room as usual. The sitter will come in today to help.

The activity table will consist of textured construction paper, magazine cut up pictures, paint/brushes, newspapers, magazines, sharpies, tape, scissors, stickers, cut out designs, stencils, and glue on the table. This is a nonverbal activity using meditation music to allow everyone to think about what they are grateful for, learning how to express themselves. for the bus. We will finished the assignment later tonight. Mr. Shoe is leaves with the tots and the buses comes for student pick-ups. Now I have a moment to myself, and head upstairs dressed up and ready to go. *La-La* and the girls will be landing soon, and she will text me when she has the luggage. I must arrive on time. My arrival time to the airport was perfect because they were waiting outside as I pull up. We are heading to the Shoe Store to work on the fashion Review all afternoon; after a quick stop for a bit to eat.

We are working hard on getting the models fitted for the runway looks. *La-La* and I will have bonding time later as the venders are arriving to deliver the inventory. The store owns a twenty-seat passenger van, basically a minibus that allows the family to travel together. Mr. Shoe made sandwiches for an afterschool snack and other treats and water. We spent the next five hours rehearsing. The adults all have a role to play for tomorrow including-Grandpa. We are expecting a large crowd tomorrow so all hands-on deck with employees and volunteers; will be working today and tomorrow. The rehearsal went well, which means less work for tomorrow. We are finally headed home for dinner and the group projects. On Friday's the master schedule board reads: Free Time, Family Fun, Whatever Needs to Be Done Time, Your Choice! I put the toddlers to bed, while the family enjoys a night of fun; until it is time to say… good night!

Saturday

Praise the Universe for another day to be alive and here with my sister. We are up early just because. La-La want to about planning a trip to somewhere tropical. I explained the visual board system to La-La, she was asking how it works. I'm planning to manufacture three types of communication boards, and sell them in the store after parent workshops. My sister loves the idea and suggests I market the boards to teachers. She will be my first customer and one put one in her kitchen.

Time waits for no one; it's time get up dressed and ready to go. We have a busy day with two shows, 3:00pm and 6:00pm. Each show takes an hour from start to finish. We are having snack trays with and a variety of cheese, crackers, fruit, and strawberry water for the guest. The easel board outside the store reads:

You Are Invited
Color for My Shoes
Spring Fashion Trends for Kids
by Mark
TODAY ONLY!
Two Shows
Three o'clock and Six o'clock

All in-store purchases today receive a 15% discount

Refreshments served

The family arrives at the shoe store at 9:00am to meet the volunteers and finalize the last-minute things. La La and I will focus on the backstage, getting the models dressed and out on the runway. Mr. Shoe will focus on the store making sure the volunteers are in position to greet the guess. It's time for the fashion review. Guess have arrived and is not seated. This is the first fashion show for the store and many more to come. We are all a little nervous but excited. But everyone is ready to walk the runway after practicing all morning. I zoned out for a minute to focus on my opening statement as the narrator.

Welcome to color for my shoes, a fall fashion review by Mark. He offers a beautiful range of children's wear using fabrics that are durable, and stylish for girls, boys, and teens that will last for many seasons. Mark's fashion for kids offers a unique style and color combination than any other designer in the fashion industry. Children's fashion is taking over the runways with seasonal themes and apparel you can take home after the show. This fall line is inspired from the radical youth movements of the 1930's. A defiant yet sophisticated look with references from the vanguard realms of art and design.

That's what Mark wanted me to say along with announcing the color themes as the models come out. I added *Princess Hiking Boots* and *Shoes For* Me to the show because they need this experience too. As the models come out, I give a description of the clothing and pointed out the color scheme. At the end of the show all the models came out to take a bow to the audience as they walked around promoting the clothing line. Both shows were a huge success and the clothing line sold out. They audience wanted to know when is the next Show and how can their child participate. I called Mark after the last sale, he asked me to inform him of the results. He was quite pleased over the attendance and sales. We agreed that his clothing line sells out with a fashion show, and he will ship a small order on Monday for the store. Mark is a new designer for children clothing, inspired by Japanese culture that he grew up in. Everyone is so excited, spring has sprung! We dropped the kids off at home with the sitter then take off for a night of celebrating a job well done.

Sunday

I've waited all week for Sunday to do nothing, my mind is programed for this. I live for Sundays but this Sunday will be different. I wake up and meditate for as long as it takes to feel a connection to the Universe. Then I read prayers for world peace. on earth. Today I've planned something special for the family so, I'm up early. I've rearranged and preplanned a dinner party for today. I want to do something special before my sister and nieces return to their home. It will be a catered semi-formal dinner. This will give the children an opportunity to learn about formal dressing. Then give them an opportunity to practice what to do at the dinner table. The dinner will take place in the dining room. First, I will give a mini lesson on formal and semi-formal attire. I never taught the children how to dress for this occasion. A formal dinner is an experience to remember. The colors and décor promote a festive atmosphere. Most formal celebrations are for special occasions like weddings, graduations, company dinners, or black-tie event. I am creating a moment in time and giving my family a memorable event right at home. The dinner will have a romantic theme and a table set for twenty. There is always something special about a combination of food, family, and a beautiful table setting. This dinner is a surprise for everyone and will start at 4:00pm. I am making calls this morning while everyone is still asleep to confirm setup and prep time. I'm planning to take everyone out for a light brunch to clear the house before the cooks and coordinators arrive. The theme is love so it's hearts, balloons, red, white, pink colors. Yes, I won't forget the dark chocolate! Everyone must wear red shoes with white or red dresses for the girls/ladies, and black suits and shoes with white, red, or pink shirts for the boys/men.

On the way back home, I tell everyone about a presentation I'm having. They must go straight to the theater when we walk in the door. I explain, today is an opportunity to learn about dining etiquette for the near future. Also, having manners when in public and at the dinner table. They should know the importance of standards when eating. I start the lecture by explaining the importance of table manners and how it helps to make a good first impression. There are visible signs of a proper table setting such as, the order of eating and what is served in a dinner course. I explained the etiquette rules and why it's important to know them before a formal dinner. Explaining dinner standards is one more know the children don't want to hear about, but I continued since standards are a part of our American culture. I give everyone a handout about what to wear and a list to follow for the next step after presentation. I arranged for a rental shop to come over and fit everyone in formal attire. All the girls are getting excited because they're dressing up for no reason, so they think. The next step is learning the dress code for a formal event. Which requires people to wear dressy clothes to a formal dinner. Such as, back-tie attire for boys/men, and morning dresses for girls/women. I talk about an old English term used for evening dress and the meaning of the black-tie attire worn on formal occasions; each style embodies sophistication. I wanted the children to know what to expect when attending a formal dinner today.

A Formal Dinner Table Setting

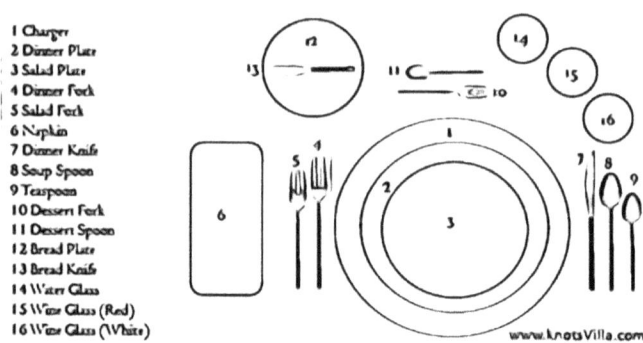

1 Charger
2 Dinner Plate
3 Salad Plate
4 Dinner Fork
5 Salad Fork
6 Napkin
7 Dinner Knife
8 Soup Spoon
9 Teaspoon
10 Dessert Fork
11 Dessert Spoon
12 Bread Plate
13 Bread Knife
14 Water Glass
15 Wine Glass (Red)
16 Wine Glass (White)

www.knotsVilla.com

Formal Wear for Men/Boys

1. Black Dinner Jacket
2. Black Trousers
3. Red Waistcoat
4. White Dress Shirt
5. Black Silk Tie
6. Black Patent Leather Shoes

Formal Ware for Women/Girls

1. Red or White formal Dress
2. Feathers (optional)
3. Gloves (optional)
4. Patent Leather or Plain Shoes
5. Pumps (shoes with heels)
6. Stockings

The next topic is about the dinner table setting and dining etiquettes. When I give presentation to the children, which are once a month they are disengaged at times so I make it exciting for them. Somewhere in the back of their mind it registers because they always have questions at the end. I give out a cheat sheet for the dinner table as a reference if someone forgets the rules.

Dinner Etiquette Rules

- Follow the dress code requested on the invitation or suggested by the host/hostess.

- Arrive at least 10 minutes early but never late!

- It's a standard to bring a small gift for the host/hostess: flowers, candy, wine, or dessert.

- Wait for the host/hostess to seat you before you sit down (there could be name cards on the table for a seating arrangement). Seating is typically, man-woman-man-woman as the women will always be to the right of a man.

- A prayer blessing, or toast is customary and done before the meal is starts.

- Always join in with a toast, if the host stands up everyone stands.

- Serving tea or coffee at the end of a meal signifies that the formal part of the evening is over. Guests may now feel free to leave, or linger if the host makes an announcement about other activities.

- After a formal dinner party, a thank you note should be sent to the host.

Table Manners

- Unfold your napkin and place it on your lap. When you are finished, place it loosely on the table not on the plate and never on your chair.

- Keep elbows off the table, and keep your left hand in your lap unless you are using it.

- Do not talk with your mouth full, chew with your mouth closed.

- Guests should do their best to mingle and make light conversation with everyone, do not talk too much or loudly. Give others equal opportunities for conversation, and talk about cheerful and pleasant things only at the dinner table.

- Don't clean up spills with your own napkin, and don't touch items that have dropped on the floor. You can use your napkin to protect yourself from spills then let your server know there is a spill.

- Loud eating noises, slurping or burping are very Impolite and the number one sin of dinner table etiquette!

- Do not blow your nose at the dinner table, excuse yourself and go to the restroom. Don't forget to wash your hands before returning.

- If you cough, cover your mouth with your napkin to stop The spread of germs and muffle the noise. If your cough becomes unmanageable, excuse yourself from the table. Wash your hands before returning to the dining table.

- Turn off your cell phone, switch it to silent mode before arriving to the table. Then leave it in your pocket or purse. It is impolite to answer a phone during dinner. If you must make or take a call, excuse yourself from the table and step outside of the dining area.

- Do not use a toothpick or apply makeup at the table.

- Say, excuse me or I'll be right back before leaving the table. Do not say that you are going to the restroom.

- When a woman leaves the table or returns to sit, all men seated with her should stand up.

- Do not push your dishes away from you or stack them for the waiter when you are finished. Leave plates and glasses where they are.

Serving Food

- Food is served from the left and dishes are removed from the right.
- Always say please when asking for something, and be sure to say thank you to your server after removing used items.
- Butter, spreads, or dips should be transferred from the serving dish to your plate before spreading or eating.

Passing Dishes or Food

- Pass food from the left to the right and do not reach over guest for things you need.
- If someone asks for the salt or pepper, pass both together even if they ask for only one item.
- When passing items (salt and pepper shakers, a breadbasket, or a butter plate) put them directly on the table instead of passing from hand to hand.
- Never intercept a pass.
- Always use serving utensils to serve yourself, not your personal silverware.

Eating

- Do NOT talk with food in your mouth! This is very rude and distasteful to watch! Wait until you have swallowed the food before speaking.
- Always taste your food first before asking for salt. Usually the host has sample the food before serving to make sure it's tasty. It's very rude to add salt and pepper before tasting your food, never assume it's tasteless.
- Don't blow on your food to cool it. If it's too hot to eat wait until it cools.
- Always scoop food by using the proper utensil.
- Cut only enough food for the next mouthful.
- Eat in small bites then chew slowly.

- If you have dietary restrictions let your host know in advance.

- It's inappropriate to request food other than what's being served by the host at a private dinner.

- Do not play with your food or utensils, and never wave or point with them. Do not hold food on utensils while talking.

- Try to pace eating so that you don't finish before others are halfway through eating. If you are a slow eater, try to speed up on so you don't keep everyone waiting. Never continue to eat long after others have stopped.

- Once the utensils are used or touched, they must never be placed on the table again. Place them inside your plate or bowl.

I know it's a lot of information all at one, but the family needs to know basic formalities of etiquettes before the formal dinner. After reading the rules, I discuss what a formal meal consists of. There are several meal courses between three to twelve options, depending on the occasion. Food courses typically includes serving salad as the first course, cheese and fruit are an optional second course. The third course is two smaller meals or one main meal. A selection of drinks must compliment the meal making it the fourth course, and yes dessert is the final and fifth serving course. Without telling everyone what's for dinner I show an example of the menu on the screen. They all yell, "I'm hungry"!

The Formal Dinner Menu

- 1st Course - Appetizers are bite size morsels that are available when you arrive for snacking and mingling while other guests arrive. Appetizers should be easy to pick up with a tooth pick to eat with one hand.

- 2nd Course - Cocktails, soft drinks, and punch is served as guest arrives to compliment the appetizers.

- 3rd Course – Soup, salad, and a breadbasket is served after the guest are seated. Indicating that all guests have arrived, and seated at the table. Soup can be hot or chilled yet light and refreshing. A small plate of baby greens/salad with vinaigrette, or a Caesar dressing is ok. White, wheat, and French bread served with butter, or coconut oil, as water and wine is served.

- 4th Course - The main course is now served with a large protein dish, and two vegetables are served with rice or potatoes for the side dish. Several meat options are available; stake, chicken, or fish. Also a vegetarian and vegan dish is available upon request and water, wine, coffee is refilled.

- 5 th Course – A light and refreshing dessert tray includes; ice cream scoops, fruit crumble, cake bites or a platter of smaller treats: dark chocolate truffles, fruit, and dark chocolate dipped strawberries served with coffee, and tea.

Presentation over! I direct everyone to go immediately upstairs to their rooms and keep doors closed until further instructions. The rental store is here to drop off and fit everyone into formal attire, everyone waits for a knock on the door. They will choose from a selection of dresses, tuxedos, accessories, and shoes. While everyone is upstairs the planners and cooks continue preparing for our arrival downstairs. I sit by the steps to prevent anyone from coming down. As everyone gets dressed, they come out in the hall for a runway walk. "Very nice", I tell them. Then everyone goes back in their rooms and wait for a second knock on the door. The planners know the dinner is a surprise, so they are careful not to ruin it. I will receive a text message to come down for a taste test to approve the décor arrangement. During that time, I knock on doors and just like magic they all open at once. Everyone comes out for photos and the photographer takes individual pictures upstairs. Then we go downstairs for the group photo when I get a text that reads, taste test is READY! I met the cook at the bottom of the stairs to taste a small portion of everything, excellent! Keeping this secret from Mr. Shoe and La-La is difficult because I do need their help. Dinner music starts playing smooth jazz and that's my cue. Everyone looks amazing as we line up in the hallway and head down stairs. They want to know why the music is playing, who's cooking food in the kitchen, are we having a formal dinner after the group photo?

After the photo we walk into an oasis of beauty in the dining room. The smell of a good meal makes everyone smile in silence. I am breathless… Everyone looks puzzled so I explain, "Today I wanted to do something special for my family to show how much I love and appreciate each one of you". The host takes each person to their seat then I make an announcement, "Welcome to your formal dinner party". I heard lots of "Wow, thank you mom, I love you mom, you're the best mom ever, I knew it, this is so nice honey!" Everyone was handed the *Dining Etiquette Rules* sheet. The host gave everyone a little pink gift bag of chocolates with a note from me that said, I love you. Follow the etiquette rules, I announce, and if you don't the host will give you a warning and place an X next to your name on your check off list. You will be graded on your performance of the *Dining Etiquette Rules.* A winner will be announced during the fifth dinner course (dessert) and will receive the big red box on the floor. What's inside will make a kid's dream come true, there is an adult gift box too. For the kids I put the latest tech toys and gift card for shoes. The adults will win a laptop and gift card for shoes. Both gift cards are from Lord and Taylor's shoe department. I remember my glamour night at the awards dinner in middle school. I received a gift card to Lord and Taylor's shoe. A memory I will never forget. That was the best in life, and I want my family to feel the way I did. I'm watching everyone being checking their etiquette sheet and watching their behaviors. Mr. Shoe felt like entertaining the table with riddles and the host gave him an X on his sheet and wrote, no joking at the dinner table Thank you! As the courses are served everyone's excited to eat their favorite meal and desserts. I must admit, this was the best formal dinner ever with my family. As dessert was served, I was handed a white envelope to announce the winner, *"Anaya"* I announced. My niece is the winner, and I am so happy for her. The show is officially over, and everyone runs upstairs to bed. Tomorrow is Monday!

Monday

Another week is here and time to live in the moment that cycles around and around. Life is for the living, and the world lives on from day to day. *La-La* and the girls are leaving today, and I will miss them. The house awakes early today. I let *La-La* a observe the routines and display board in each room. To my surprise, everyone was up and focused on the time. Downstairs, breakfast time, lunch bags in the backpacks, bags at the door, busses come and go. Mr. Shoe; turn to drop the toddlers Off. My sister and I will spend a the day relaxing planning for a family vacation. I need to recover from the dinner expenses before any financial commitments. *La-La* wanted to plan for December, but next year will be better. I want something out of the country maybe visit to the family's village in Africa, the Caribbean, or South America would be nice too. *La-La* said she will plan everything, and we will decide in three months. So, months later we talk about the who, what, when, where, and why. Something that will accommodate a large group. Somewhere relaxing, calming elements, and a beach for sure. *La-La* flight leaves at 9:00pm, so we are just hanging out at home.

Spending time with family that love you unconditionally, makes me feel happy. All the memories and experiences of growing up, become stories that are passed on to the next generation. I'm focusing on creating more bonding activities with family, to strengthen our legacy. It is my duty to promote family pride and bonding. To create opportunities for family reunions, which is a way to know who's who to build a connection. The entire family from all branches is need and should want to make a commitment to family. Supporting ideas, having stability, building wealth, and having a foundation for future generations. We talked about getting family to communicate, start businesses, and travel together. It's all about the actions of each family member. The theme for this family reunion is to ask, where do we go from here, and what will we leave the next generation? Not only will the family get together for fun, but we also share ideas and unite. This week I will give the children tips on how to connect and stay connected with other family members that they don't know. *La-La* and I are organizing a family pen-pal activity for everyone (children and adults) before the family vacation. Getting to know all family members before seeing them is important.

Happy New Year!

A year is long, but it comes and goes, and La-La is planning the family vacation for this year. She will contact family members to inform them of a family reunion. First, she creates a family content book to include names, numbers, and social media tags. Then she chooses four locations that we talked about for the family to vote on. Africa, the Caribbean, South America, or Central America; by sending an evite to every member to cast their vote. All votes are in: Africa 40, Caribbean 70, South America 25, Central America 80. Wow that's a large voting turnout and not all members voted, but they still have a chance. Now that we have numbers to work with, choosing a country in Central America will be another vote. I am happy that Central America won the vote, but I really wanted to visit South America. Mr. Shoe and I talked about visiting Brazil and maybe moving there. I want to live in another country to start a Shoe Store. If we can travel more, The Shoe family will find the right country to reside, choosing a safe place and the best location for business. For the next round of voting, I texted a map of Central America. Then asked voters to research the best country for the vacation then cast their vote again. This assignment took longer to decide, I included the children's opinion for the family vote. They worked together on a PowerPoint to present research of the pros and cons of each country in Central America. We learned a lot about each country for the best experience and the most fun. The decision was based on safety, touring options, and a beach front. Central America looks amazing along the narrow land mass between Mexico and South America. It would be nice to visit other countries within the region, too expensive but worth it. I'm interested in Panama or Costa Rica. So, after the presentation everyone voted, and Costa Rica is the winner.

Costa Rica occupies a privileged spot in the heart of Central America, while its territory covers 19,652 square miles and touches both the Atlantic and Pacific oceans. The country is accessible and expensive due to its location. The smaller vacation destinations are usually more costly and Costa Rica is very popular. The travel from coast to coast is three hours by car or 45 minutes by plane. The Caribbean region of Costa Rica stands out for its variety of aquatic ecosystems, and its beautiful white and black sandy beaches. It provides water activities like sport fishing, scuba diving, jet skiing, and Snorkeling. The beaches are very popular as expected. Americas are permitted to enter the country without a visa and a maximum stay up to 90 days.

Other votes came in for Costa Rica, Panama, Belize, El Salvador, and Mexico, wow this is going to be hard. The two counties with the most votes are Costa Rica and Belize. La La and I thought realistically, looking at the numbers and Costa Rica here we come. The Caribbean side of Costa Rica is tropical and the country is located between 8 - 11 degrees north of the Equator. There are two seasons, rainy and dry. The dry season starts December to April and the rainy season May to November. Seasonal changes in temperatures bring major weather concerns. Although nights are cooler in some areas during the rainy season, Mornings are sunny all year. Now we can start a pricing package for the family reunion Vacation. Of course, a monthly payment plan is included. I will explore Brazil on another trip for shoe business possibilities. Costa Rica is a smaller country servicing mainly tourism. After the PowerPoint presentation We looked at YouTube videos of Costa Rica. I ask the children," what do they think about moving to another country", That was a big NO. They are all worried about their friends and that it will feel different. That's something I must consider.

The goal of the shoe business is to network with people and companies in the industry for the global marketplace. The next step towards the vacation is to look for Airbnb homes or hotels that will accommodate a large group. The area we will reside in after researching Is Manuel Antonio National Park. The park has a wonderful combination of a rain forest, beaches, and coral reefs. The beaches are known to be the most beautiful in the country. The rain forest is home of sloths, the rare and adorable squirrel monkeys, iguanas, and millions of colorful little crabs. The homes in the area are humongous and sleeps up to thirty-five people and have windows with a view. Every room surrounds an area of the park Including the beach. We can cook our own food and save money by not eating out every night or hire a chef. I can't wait to enjoy a cup of locally grown coffee, then watch the Titi Monkeys jump from one treetop to another. The big windows allow an ocean breeze to enter as the spectacular views, and the abundance of nature surrounds the homes that create pure serenity. This location in Costa Rica provides several opportunities for fun and one of the best areas that provides a piece of mind. I think everyone will be happy with the location.

With a group rate on Nature Airlines we put together a price package that includes a tour plan, meals per day, and ground transportation. The family group will fly into San Jose, Pavas International Airport, with a bus ride to Manuel Antonio National Park. Everyone will receive four vacation options to choose a plan that fits their budget and situation. Then we need a total number of vacation plans to coordinate the daily transportation for the total package price. The tour plans are a must do. The available tour packages are:

The Adventure Package includes: Costa Rica's rugged natural terrain for those seeking a week of non-stop fun and a bit of adrenaline like; explosive volcanoes, rushing rapids, remote jungle lodges, and rainforest canopies. We will see how many of the young people sign up for this.

- 10 days and 9 nights in 3 fabulous Costa Rica hotels, $1,200 per person, domestic flights and ground transfers.

The Romantic Package includes: Costa Rica is for lovers and nature lovers. This package is perfect for honeymooners, anniversaries, or just a romantic vacation. Surround by the rainforest, volcanoes, and beaches to get in touch with nature as you visit a remote indigenous Village. A visit with a medicine man for natural herbs to treat and heal pain. Enjoy the peaceful nights in a cabin elevated over the ocean!

- 9 days and 8 nights in 3 fabulous Costa Rica hotels, $1,100.00. Guided Volcano Tour, Rainforest Zip Line Adventure, Tortuga Island Snorkeling and Beach Adventure, Coffee Plantation Tour.

Leisure Package includes: A retreat to the forest or relax on the beach, this leisure itinerary features; lazy days, comfortable accommodations that allow you to sleep in, and watch the worries of the modern world melt away. Costa Rica's beautiful shorelines are tucked away in verdant Jungles creating a harmonic, and natural ambience that is calming and cozy. Hide from technology in a remote Eco lodge or chill out with a therapeutic massage on the beach.

- 9 days/8 nights, $1,200 per person, a quiet Island retreat (electronics not allowed).

No Stress No Worry Package includes: A ten bedroom private home snuggled in the hills of Manuel Antonio National Park surrounded by mountain peaks in this spacious guest house. With an open bar, an all you can eat treat to enjoy entertainment on a balcony overlooking the beach. Electronics are available, a PlayStation and other gaming systems, movie channels, and a beach day everyday adventure. No schedules, no guided tours, and nothing to look forward too unless you created it.

- 10 days and 9 nights $2,500.00 US airfare, amenities, and transportation included.

La-La will take over the planning where I left off. She will continue by sending out a survey for a vote on the package plans. I'm interested in the, no stress no worry package for my family and add the adventure package. All the tour packages sound great but with a large family our international vacations are limited. It took every month of year to plan this reunion and here we come Costa Rica. I'm getting an early start on packing. I get anxiety when it's time to fly in the friendly skies (so they say). I keep myself stress-free during this process. Mr. Shoe plans to meet with a company in Brazil to discuss shoe business. The businessman has a shoe franchise in the U.S., and wants to help us with opening a Store in Brazil. It sounds exciting, and if the meeting goes well Mr. Shoe will leave for Brazil and meet us in Costa Rica. The voting numbers are huge, this planning is more than a notion. The final count for the tour packages are in, so *La-La* grouped the numbers by tour package accordingly. The lodge is the main guest house where the family will gather for meetings, activities, the meet up for the tour buses, or just an open house between tours. The guess lodge has all the amenities we need except a menu and food. So, each family will organize a day to cook when we all gather for entertainment, family stories, parties, and fun.

The time is now, it time put together the last minutes items in carry-ons, the check-in luggage is locked. Tomorrow we are up and off for a journey that creates memories. We find ourselves landing in San Jose, Costa Rica into a new world. Seeing the landscape of the small country is simply beautiful during aerial views as we land. Natural beauty is humbling, as it takes my breath away during the decent, touchdown! I say my prayers, praising the Universe for allowing the plane to land safely. Mr. Shoe will meet the us here in Costa Rica tomorrow, so I traveled with family members to help. The temperature is warm but not blazing hot. The tropical feeling sets the tone for perfect vacation weather. Everyone is hungry by now, so we wait for our luggage then load the busses that are waiting for us outside. "Welcome to San Jose, Costa Rica" I tell the group. As our tour of the city begins with sightseeing on the way to restaurant for pizza. We ordered and prepaid lunch that *La-La* organized upon arrival. Pizza in Costa Rica sounds good, it's quick and easy to serve on the busses. Each bus is given additional informational by the driver during the 3-hour tour to Manuel Antonio National Park, final destination. All I can think about in this moment is spending the next ten days living life to the fullest, in the abundance of the rainforest.

Before everyone gets off the buses at our destination, I recommend relaxing and enjoying the journey of sightseeing during the road trip. My family will host a backyard barbeque at the lodge, the food was prearranged and will be cooked upon our arrival. I surprised everyone with something on the grill, cold salads, baked beans, grilled corn on the cob, potato salad, coleslaw, burgers, hot dogs, ribs, chicken wings, deviled eggs, watermelon, apple pie, vanilla ice cream, and chocolate chip cookies, brownies, and beverages. The moment I woke up I sensed a feeling of elation and felt so free (as a bird) as my prefrontal cortex started releasing serotonin. I took a deep breath and suddenly I was… flying! I come downstairs to a party. Music playing and everyone's dancing to the rhythm of Costa Rican's Latin beat. I can't believe I'm in this moment, I'm here, I feel so good right now. After a restful night all groups were picked up at designated location for the family reunion at the lodge. The family said morning for prayer, ate breakfast, and a group game; before our first adventure in Manuel Antonio National Park. The guide leads us with history of the park before the tour, the groups will split off to their adventure package plans or other excursions.

This park is South of Quepos on the Pacific Coast, 132 km from San José. It is so popular because of its expensive white sand beaches backed by an evergreen forest that grows right up to the high tide line. The habitants in the park are primary forest, secondary forest, mangrove swamps, lagoons and beach vegetation. There is a varied fauna with 109 species of mammals and 184 species of birds. The park includes 12 little Isles just off the coast, dolphins and migrating whales can be observed too. Ponce de León, the Spanish explorer, whose futile search for the Fountain of Youth became his signature expedition (finding this area in 1519) that is rarely recognized for one of his greatest discoveries; the Quepos and Manuel Antonio area".

It's important to know the history of the places once visited because it can leave a lasting memory. We packed lunches to have a picnic before choosing one of the many activities after the tour.

Titi Canopy

ATV Tours

Mangrove Tours

Sport fishing

Mountain Biking

Rivers Rafting

Bird Watching

Rainmaker

Surfing

Diving Tours

Sunset Sails Tours

Nature Farm

Play Tennis

Golf Tour

Canyon Tour

Damas Caves

Jet Ski Tour

Spices Tour

The are several restaurants to host the family's farewell dinner. My family votes on one of the tours for today; rivers rafting, bird watching, nature farm, rainmaker are the most popular.

Rivers Rafting - This tour is a great way to see the beauty and wonders of the rainforest in Costa Rica. Take a trip deep into the jungle for an adventure on one of the cleanest rivers in Central America. There is time for a short hike to see the amazing waterfalls, swim and explore the area. During May through December the rapid waves is like a roller coaster, but the waves in the dry season December through April offers more of a mellow ride.

Includes light breakfast, lunch, transportation, professional guides and equipment

Tour Times: 7:30am and 12:00pm.

Bird Watching - You will notice flocks of brown pelicans gracefully soaring overhead. Then plunging into the sea after fish. How about wind surfing as they playfully glide along the face of a wave with a wingtip, almost skimming the wall of water. The magnificent frigate birds large dark wings are long and forked tails will grab your attention as they effortlessly cruise on the slightest breeze. If you love birds, you know that most species are not as easily seen as pelicans and frigate birds. But they can be found in the Manuel Antonio Park that harbor hundreds of them. More than 270 species including migrants, can potentially be observed in the park and the surrounding area extending to Quepos and the local airstrip.

Includes transportation, professional guides, Tour Times: 9:00am only.

Nature Farm - This project is part of a 25 year commitment to protect this unique 30 acre tropical forest connected by natural tree corridors to the nearby Manuel Antonio National Park. The reserve features a Butterfly Garden and a special evening of sound and image presentations called the Symphony of Nature. You will have the opportunity to spot many species of local birds, troops of Howler, white faced, and Titi monkeys, with many species of tropical flora, including the 200 years old hardwood trees from England and Spain. The tour guide recommends comfortable shoes, ponchos, and binoculars.

1. The Butterfly Botanical Gardens is a uniquely designed garden atrium with plant and insect exhibits. Duration: 1 hour.

2. The Nature Interpretative Walk and Aquatic Tropical Gardens features a variety of local Flora and Fauna. Duration: 2 hours.

3. The Butterfly Botanical Gardens and Nature Walk, combination. Duration: 2.5 hours.

4. Jungle Night Walk is a unique odyssey into the nocturnal world of the tropical rainforest. Visit the amphibian water gardens, and listen to the nightlife of over a dozen species of frogs. Tour Time: 8:00pm Duration: 50 minutes.

Rainmaker- Rainmaker Mountain is one of the last remnants of primary rainforest in the Central Pacific. It is home to 60% of all the flora and fauna species found in Costa Rica. This private reserve is dedicated to the conservation and protection of the Fila Chonta Mountain range on Costa Rica's pacific side. Rainmaker's unique location places it within a biological corridor. This area is protected to ensure that future generations to come will enjoyed it too. Presumed extinct in Costa Rica, the Harlequin toad has been rediscovered in the Rainmaker reserve in 2003. The poison toad's distinctive yellow and black markings, believed to ward off predators, once made it easy to identify when the species populated Costa Rican and Panamanian streams. The astonishing view of the coastline, mountain streams, waterfalls, and the magnificence of its rainforest makes the Rainmaker an essential destination for nature lovers. The tour includes natural juices, fresh fruits snacks, a typical Costa Rican lunch, and round trip transportation from the Quepos Manuel Antonio.

Recommended to bring: walking shoes, light clothes, bathing suit, binoculars and a camera. Self-guided tours: 8:00am

Mr. Shoe made his round trip to Brazil and back to Costa Rita to join us with a contract in his hand, #yeah. We went on three of the tours and experienced bird watching, nature farm, and rainmaker. The children were amazed with the tours and can't stop talking about them. This experience opened their senses, gave them a better understanding about our Universe, awareness of nature, and what it means to all species. I saw a different side of my children, they were quiet and very attentive throughout the tour. They asked questions and put their hands on everything that was friendly to touch. Nature is a beautiful feeling as it provides a calming element for all humans, animals, and creatures by giving all living things a since of being. I gave out supply bags and journals to create a scrapbook after collecting items from each tour. Then the journals were used to express how they saw nature (a birds eye view). The time we spent absorbing another part of world and relaxing in the wonders of nature, added gratitude and appreciation to our lives as a family. We appreciate one another more, we will stay in touch share more, and love more for the sake of family and After a long ten days it's time to pack up and go back home. The reality of living in paradise is now over and the great escape has come the end. I could stay longer and I'm sure everyone would agree. It's hard to say good bye to yesterday as we are on route to the airport. I close my eyes for the next three hours and meditated into a deep sleep. I wake up at the airport and go through the process of boarding the flight, then I sleep again. This time when I wake up and I'm in a daze from my dream world and realize I'm home. I get in bed and continue where I left off, reminiscing about paradise.

www.ingramcontent.com/pod-product-compliance
Lightning Source LLC
Chambersburg PA
CBHW051526120626
46551CB00012B/1097

9 781960 952028